GOD WITH US

Cowley Publications is a ministry of the Society of Saint John the Evangelist, a religious community of men in the Episcopal Church. Emerging from the Society's tradition of prayer, theological reflection, and diversity of mission, the press is centered in the rich heritage of the Anglican Communion.

Cowley Publications seeks to provide books, audio cassettes, CDs, and other resources for the ongoing theological exploration and spiritual development of the Episcopal Church and others in the body of Christ. To this end, it is dedicated to developing a new generation of theological writers, encouraging them to produce timely, creative, and stimulating publications of excellence, and making these publications available widely, reaching both clergy and lay persons.

GOD WITH US

THE COMPANIONSHIP OF JESUS
IN THE CHALLENGES OF LIFE

Herbert O'Driscoll

COWLEY PUBLICATIONS
Cambridge, Massachusetts

Published in the United Sates of America by Cowley Publications, a division of the Society of Saint John the Evangelist. No portion of this book may be reproduced, stored in or introduced into a retrieval system, or transmitted, in any form or by any means—including photocopying—without the prior written permission of Cowley Publications, except in the case of brief quotations embedded in critical articles and reviews.

Library of Congress Cataloging-in-Publication Data:
O'Driscoll, Herbert.
    God with us : the companionship of Jesus in the challenges of life / Herbert O'Driscoll.
        p. cm.
    Includes index.
        ISBN 1-56101-208-4
    I. Christian life. II. Title.
BV4501.3 .O37 2002
242—dc21   2002013715

Scripture quotations are taken from The New Revised Standard Version of the Bible, © 1989, by the Division of Christian Education of the National Council of the Churches of Christ in the United States of America. Used by permission.

Cover photograph: The cover image is "Mystic Christ" courtesy of and © 1999 Fr. John Giuliani. Color reproductions of this image are available from Bridge Building Images: *www.BridgeBuilding.com*
Cover design: Jennifer Hopcroft

This book was printed in the United States of America on acid-free paper.

Cowley Publications
907 Massachusetts Avenue
Cambridge, Massachusetts 02139
800-225-1534   *www.cowley.org*

CONTENTS

PREFACE

If there is one thing that Christians can say with confidence in today's world, it is the age old statement: Jesus lives.

The evidence for this is remarkable, and all the more so for the number of people unaware of it. Books of every kind are being published about Jesus, by no means all of them in the world of religious publishing. Many people outside the church are fascinated by his life and teaching. The number of those who acknowledge him as Lord of their lives is exploding, especially outside Western culture in the worlds of Asia, Africa, and South America.

In Western culture itself, wary as it may be about any institutional form of Christian faith, there is a longing that is almost palpable. Where Jesus of Nazareth can be found to be addressing the realities of contemporary life, there is a wish to know more of him.

At the heart of Christian faith is the claim that, in Jesus of Nazareth, God lived a fully human life among us. In that human life he encountered the full spectrum of experience that each one of us experiences. There were those whom he loved and those who loved him. There was all the stress of a very public life. There were in abundance hopes and disappointments, moments of a sense of achievement and moments of a sense of failure. These things, and much more that we know from our own human journey, were known and felt in our Lord's life. To know that we have Jesus as companion in our daily living can be immensely strengthening, especially in times of challenge and stress. My hope is that these pages will help to forge that companionship.

Speaking of companions makes me realize how much I owe to Robert Maclennan for his continued guidance and assistance through many manuscripts. He has for long helped to shape my hastily written prose, adding a trifle here, excising a little there. My manuscripts have been the better for his years of experience as an editor, and I thank him.

Since these reflections may sometimes be useful to those of us, clergy and lay, who speak to others in his name, scriptural references are provided in an Index at the back of the book.

—HERBERT O'DRISCOLL
Pentecost 2002

BEGINNINGS

How do we identify the moment when something begins? When did we begin to know what we wanted to become in life? When did we begin to fall in love with someone? When did a certain movement in national life begin? When did the modern world begin?

When did Christianity begin? In one sense we can be very precise: it began when a child was born in Bethlehem. But did it? Or did it begin when a young woman said "yes" to a divine messenger who spoke to her deepest being? Did it begin outside time and history entirely, in the realm from which the messenger was sent? Each of the four gospel writers makes a different choice of what they consider the beginning. Mark opens with the appearance of John the Baptizer in the Judean wilderness. Matthew traces the line of a family back through no less than forty-two generations, before letting us meet the young virgin Mary in Nazareth. Luke starts by introducing us to the aging parents of John the Baptizer before the birth of their child. John the Evangelist begins by taking us on a journey to the heart of the universe and the beginning of time, where we see Jesus as the companion of the Creator, involved in the process of the creation of the universe.

This small book attempts to link events in the gospels with events in our daily lives, to find points of similarity and messages of hope. Those gospel events are far larger than our daily lives and are capable of endless meanings not plumbed in these few pages. But we who read the gospels are entitled to ask that they speak to the joys and sorrows and challenges of our human experience.

There was a prelude to the beginning of the life of Jesus, just as there was to our own lives. His mother became conscious of the visitation of a messenger. She went through the experience of giving birth in difficult circumstances. She experienced not only the crises of bringing up a child but also fear and danger from a tyrannical regime. Those circumstances formed Jesus, as our parents and our childhood formed us. They were a prelude to the kind of human being he became and the choices he eventually made in his life—choices that were made at dreadful cost, but that have glorified and inspired our humanity for ever.

1

EXPLORING NEW POSSIBILITIES

In the sixth month the angel Gabriel was sent by God to a town in Galilee called Nazareth, to a virgin espoused to a man whose name was Joseph, of the house of David. The virgin's name was Mary. And he came to her and said, "Greetings, favored one! The Lord is with you." But she was much perplexed by his words, and pondered what sort of greeting this might be. The angel said to her, "Do not be afraid Mary, for you have found favor with God. And now you will conceive in your womb and bear a son, and you will name him Jesus."

(Luke 1:26–31)

Within each of us there is a country—its landscapes are as varied as the outer landscapes that we travel, sometimes beautiful and captivating, sometimes barren and forbidding. As with the landscapes of outer geography, there is always more to be explored in our inner life, whether the explorer is ourselves or someone else who wants to know us intimately. In fact, if our relationships both with ourselves and with others are to be healthy, our mutual exploring must never end. Every discovery is a prelude to another.

The village girl in the story is young. We are told nothing else about her at the moment when we meet her in scripture. Later, as we follow the story of her life, we will see that this young woman has an immense capacity to remain faithful under great stress. We see also that she is thought of tenderly by the spiritual giant to whom she gave the gift of birth, who calls her mother, and whom we call our Lord Jesus Christ. We know, too, that she was visited by an angel. There is nothing unusual in this. Since angels are the messengers that God sends to offer direction for our lives, each of us has been visited by angels. Sometimes we have ignored their calling, and sometimes we have heard and obeyed, setting off in the direction to which we have been pointed.

Years later, if a friend asked the woman about the moment when she felt visited, she might say only that she had received a messenger. She might describe how she felt fear in the first moments of becoming aware of a presence, how the fear passed, how she felt strangely reassured, and how then she knew that she would give birth. Perhaps she told these things to her son.

About the months of her pregnancy we know almost nothing. We assume that it went normally. However, we know that there was always some questioning of its circumstances. For instance, at an early stage in her pregnancy she felt driven to make a dangerous journey to see an older relative. Then toward the end of her pregnancy she found herself having to take an even longer and more dangerous journey, at the demand of the Roman authorities occupying her country. We know that she came to a crowded town, and that she and her husband were directed to a cave where, amid their few belongings, she gave birth to her child.

The business of an angel, like the one who came to Mary, is to point us to further exploration within ourselves. Because it comes from God, an angel can know how much in us has been brought to realization and how much more is still waiting to be explored. The angel knows and can point us to knowing what gifts given to us at birth have never yet been used. When they come to us, the messengers of God always ask us to give birth in some way. They ask us to give birth to something new in our lives—perhaps to a work of art, or to a new relationship with another, or to a time of self-discovery when we learn, sometimes with astonishment, that we are capable of things far beyond our imagining, whether it be creating something new, bearing a great burden, serving in a great cause, facing a daunting crisis, or nourishing another life.

Whatever we are called to do or to be, we will find Mary's experience speaking to our lives. And as her own child spoke to her and guided her in life, so he will speak in ours. If we ask him for grace for our journey, we will find that it is given. When, led by angelic visitation, we explore and give birth to new possibilities within us, we find meaning and vocation in our lives.

We call his mother blessed because the gift of life that she gave to her son is a prelude to the gift of life that he gives to us. We call her son our Lord because, through him, we find strength and grace for our living.

2

GRAPPLING WITH CHALLENGES

Now the birth of Jesus the Messiah took place in this way. When his mother Mary had been engaged to Joseph, but before they lived together, she was found with child by the Holy Spirit. Her husband Joseph, being a righteous man and unwilling to expose her to public disgrace, planned to dismiss her quietly. But . . . an angel of the Lord appeared to him in a dream and said "Joseph, son of David, do not be afraid to take Mary as your wife. . . . She will bear a son, and you are to name him Jesus."

(from Matthew 1:18–25)

Usually the birth of a child is greeted with joy and celebration. But there are times in some people's lives when joy and celebration at a birth are hardly possible. When a pregnancy is neither expected nor planned, the arrival of the baby may bring great consternation. Even in a good solid loving family, where there are other children and provisions for the needs of life are ample, the coming of a new child may bring stress, psychological or financial, or both.

Jesus' birth was anything but easy for the two people trying desperately to prepare for it. The mother was reeling from a pregnancy begun while she was yet unmarried. Joseph, who knew he was not the father, was grappling with the stress of the decisions he had to make. They lived in a world where the will and traditions of the community loomed large in the lives of individuals. Both Mary and Joseph must have been deeply apprehensive of how the community would react to the birth of this baby.

Suddenly, to Joseph there comes a moment of resolution and decision. It comes in a dream that challenges him to get involved in the new reality rather than to stand outside it and merely worry. "You are to name him Jesus," the dream visitor commands. For Joseph, detachment and indecision end, and responsibility and participation begin.

The words of the dream are arresting. They command our attention too. First, Joseph is told not to be afraid. Fear can be immobilizing. Fear can blow a situation out of all proportion, making it more impossible to deal with as each hour and day passes. Fear feeds on the illusion that there is no one who understands, no one to speak with, no one to help. But very often, if we reach out and find that help is available, the situation is transformed, and we can regain a sense of proportion and prepare to meet it. Second, Joseph is told to name the child that will be born. When we name a person or a thing, we fully acknowledge its reality. And when we fully acknowledge the reality of something we are facing, we are often released from the negative emotions that possess us. Then we can see it for what it is, and deal with it. A well-known example occurs in the Twelve Step program. There, naming the problem for what it really is makes possible a decisive dealing with it.

We might object at this point—wouldn't it be nice if some of the daunting decisions *we* have to make could be easily resolved by settling down to sleep and receiving the visit of a friendly angel who directs us to what we should do, and gives us the nerve to do it? Fair enough. But we should look again at this moment in Joseph's life. We can be assured that God has many ways to communicate with us, as we deal with life's challenges and questions.

Some people have had vivid experiences of direction that came quite literally in a dream. They have felt themselves to have been addressed in a deep way that they cannot ignore. Albert Einstein was one. After a long time of grappling with the question of relativity, he woke up one morning with the insight that led to the famous equation, E=mc2.

Sometimes a dream can be a waking dream, a time when we vision and imagine to ourselves all the dimensions of something that must be decided, and see in our mind's eye the costs and consequences of this or that decision. Sometimes we may decide to share the issue with a friend or a counselor. As the other listens with care, asks questions that cause us to probe deeper or view things more widely, and occasionally offers suggestions or direction, we may well have the sense of being guided by an angel.

In any of these ways of grappling with the challenges that life brings us, we are doing what Joseph was directed to do. We are choosing not to be the victims of fear. We are engaging the situation rather than seeing and feeling ourselves to be merely its victim. To choose, to act, to take hold—this can often make all the difference.

—✥3✥—

ASSESSING THE
CIRCUMSTANCES

*An angel of the Lord appeared to Joseph in a dream
and said, "Get up, take the child and his mother, and
flee to Egypt, and remain there until I tell you; for
Herod is about to search for the child, to destroy him."
Then Joseph got up, took the child and his mother by
night, and went to Egypt, and remained there until
the death of Herod.*

(Matthew 2:13–15)

✥ ✥

There are times in life when we need to assess carefully
the circumstances facing us and our ability to handle
them. If we decide that we can confront them, then we
set about doing so. We take our stand. However, we may
decide to avoid a confrontation, at least for now. Sometimes there is good reason for avoidance, and we defer
action with the hope that, at some time in the future, we
will be in a position to engage the situation with better
chance of success.

There are caves in the escarpment on which Bethlehem is built. To stand at the mouth of one of these caves,
as Joseph may have done, is to look toward the east.
There, about five miles away, is what Joseph would have
known—and probably dreaded—as the Herodium, the

mountain which Herod, a military and technical genius of his day, had transformed at enormous expense into a fortress to dominate the surrounding countryside.

Joseph has been warned that the child behind him in the cave is a threat to the aging, paranoid king. The king is known for countering perceived threat with brutal action, even within his own family. Joseph knows that if the new born child is discovered, no mercy will be shown. He decides that he must get his family to safety, and the only real safety lies in the desert to the south west. Beyond that, at the mouth of the great delta of the Nile, is the huge city of Alexandria where, Joseph knows, there is a large Jewish population. There the family may find shelter and safety.

And so, although on this journey they will only exchange an immediate danger for dangers yet unknown, they hastily gather their few possessions and set out. Dawn finds them hurrying on their way, putting distance between themselves and the threat hanging over them. Eventually they would almost certainly have attached themselves to some caravan heading toward Egypt. The road they would most likely have traveled on—the Way of the Sea—would have been the modern equivalent of a main well traveled highway.

As I watch them in imagination I feel the immense vulnerability about this couple and their child. They are anything but affluent. As ordinary, humble people they have no defense against the forces that press on them from every side. If Herod's forces catch them, they will die. If a caravan leader, having taken their fee for offered protection, then betrays them, they will be helpless. No guarantee of safety awaits them, even at their journey's end.

Millions of people in the world today face similar terrors, and many flee their homes and become refugees.

Many more face poverty, hunger, homelessness, and disease. For their own and their children's sake, they have hard decisions to make about how to keep going, how to make do, when to protest, where to find help, where to make a stand.

My situation seems very different, yet there are elements that even I share with this couple and their child. I live in a world of law and comfort among friends, family, colleagues, and neighbors. Yet I live in an economy that can be savage and unpredictable, one that regards me first as a functionary and only later as a person. I live in a stressful and demanding society that can, if I am not careful, drain my energy and damage my health. Whatever wealth I may have is hostage to the vagaries of financial forces far beyond my power to affect them or mitigate their ferocity. In a sense I, and those whom I love, travel in a wilderness. It is a wilderness very unlike the terrain through which that long-ago family passed, but even the road I travel can very quickly make me realize my vulnerability and my limitations.

Unless I decide to retreat completely from reality, I have little choice about engaging with the contemporary world. But I do have a choice as to how I engage it. If I decide to grapple with the realities, I am choosing Joseph's way—the way of engaging the situation rather than seeing and feeling myself to be its victim. In scripture I read that Joseph was enabled to do this by God's grace and direction. My prayer is that I never forget that I too have access to that same grace.

4

THE MYSTERY OF GROWING

Every year his parents went to Jerusalem for the festival of the Passover. And when he was twelve years old they went up as usual for the festival. When the festival was ended, the boy Jesus stayed behind in Jerusalem, but his parents did not know it. They returned to Jerusalem to search for him. After three days they found him in the Temple, sitting among the teachers, listening to them and asking them questions.

(from Luke 2:41–52)

Any parent who has ever lost contact with a child knows the terrible and terrifying barrage of feelings—the sudden realization of absence—the effort to take charge of the situation and not to panic—the fear that settles in as the time lengthens—the constant and tormenting recall of recent hours or days spent with the child, with the remorseful wishing that one had done this or that differently. Together with all of this, there is the weight of self-imposed guilt. Then at last, if everything works out well, there comes the desperately hoped-for discovery and the flood of mingled relief, love, and anger.

It is all here in this story. Add to the potent mixture of experience the fact that the world in which the Holy Family lived offered no means of instant communication or travel. Instead, they found themselves hours or even days away from the missing child, with no way of making contact, and the child was lost in a city teeming with unknown people from all over the world.

Meanwhile, back in the city, what must have been the feelings of this twelve year old? While we have no direct evidence, nothing suggests that he was frantic with fear. Quite the opposite, in all probability. After all, what could be more fascinating for a twelve year old, who had lived all his life in a small town far from the center of things, than to find himself in a large bustling city full of wonderful sights and sounds? We can almost see him looking about eagerly, deciding what to explore next. We are almost inclined to suspect that he had decided to stay behind.

Eventually his parents find him. The mixture of emotions known to every parent in such a situation sounds in every syllable of what they blurt out on seeing him: "Child, why have you treated us like this?" His response is typical. There is not the slightest suggestion that he has any idea of what they have been through. Instead, he asks what must have been an utterly infuriating question, "Why were you searching for me?" This is followed by an equally infuriating and patronizing, "Did you not know . . . ?" Every parent hears those words, "But, Mum and Dad, didn't you know?"—always with the implied, "How can you be so stupid!"

If we identify first with Jesus, we recognize the cost to others of the way in which our growing has taken place. Not only our youthful growing, but also the full process of our adult development. We might be surprised and pained to see our lives through the eyes of those who love us, especially through our parents' eyes. They may have had dreams for us we have not fulfilled. There may be things about our personality they find disappointing. They

may have disapproved silently of certain decisions we have
taken through the years. None of this means that we have
been, or are, any less loved. But it does mean that much
of what we take for granted ourselves has been costly to
those who love us.

When we identify with the parents in the story, mentally, emotionally, and physically drained as they must
have been, we taste the cost of parenthood. The cost is
particularly high when a child is ceasing to be a child and
becoming what we sometimes call his or her own person.
Yet this is a mysterious kind of pain or stress, because it
is also shot through with a kind of pride in what is hap-
pening. A human being is emerging into fullness, and this
human being is to some degree of our making and will
always be part of us. The process common to both child
and parent is the mystery of growth, the beautiful and
sometimes painful process of life itself.

"They did not understand," says Luke in his telling of
this very human moment. It's true. Rarely do we fully
understand one another, even those closest to us, even
ourselves. Nor can we fully understand, because the com-
plexity and subtlety of life is beyond understanding. This
is precisely why we need the grace for living that is sup-
plied by the Lord whose earthly life and experience was
fully as human as ours.

COMMUNITY

When we mentally list the riches of our lives, we rarely include what may be life's greatest gift—the communities where we live, with their many and varied relationships. Most of us know a number of communities: the neighborhood of our home, the locality of our work with its colleagues, the church where we worship, the organizations we join for sport or hobby—and this is to name only a few. There is even a new kind of community we may have found on the invisible world of the Internet. Within these places of mutual acquaintance we have a place, an identity, a home. As the years advance, we learn to treasure these circles and contribute our gifts to the life going on in them.

From the first days of his public ministry, Jesus began to gather the small circle that would soon number twelve. There was important symbolism in this. Israel was composed of twelve tribes. This circle of twelve men would embody the nucleus of the tribes of the new Israel. To call them merely disciples is not enough. So we name them "the first community." One day the church would see itself as the community of the new Israel.

Right from the beginning of Jesus' ministry a wider
community was forming beyond the circle of the disciples. Some of its first members were Jesus' friends, who,
because of their friendship with him, felt a natural affin-
ity for each other. Mary, Martha, and Lazarus of Bethany
were very early members of this community. Mary of
Magdala was certainly a member. Later on, many of those
whom Jesus encountered would surely have become
attached to him and his other followers. Someone like
Zacchaeus, for instance, whose life changed both per-
sonally and professionally—surely he would have kept up
some kind of contact after the initial encounter.

Both the circle of the disciples and the larger surrounding community were very human. They were people we would recognize in everyday life. Very few came
from the upper echelons of their society. Most of them,
like us, had to work for their living, pay their taxes—often
exorbitant—and pray that they might not fall victim to
turbulent times and to foreign rulers who could be cruel
and arbitrary.

The more we see of Jesus' disciples and the better we
get to know them, the more exasperating they can be—
constantly bickering about their standing in relation to
him and to each other, constantly failing to understand
his vision and hopes and, in the end, intent on survival
at any cost in the face of the final seeming catastrophe.
Yet all of this is good news for us latter-day disciples. If
the early days and years of the faith were built on such
ordinary, even unlikely, material, then it follows that good
things, perhaps even a few wonderful things, can be
achieved by *our* ordinary lives if we take our place in the
community and offer ourselves as best we can in alle-
giance to Jesus as Lord.

—=5=—

TIMES OF DECISION

When all the people were baptized [by John the Baptist], and when Jesus also had been baptized, the heaven was opened, and the Holy Spirit descended upon him in bodily form as a dove. And a voice came from heaven, "You are my son, the beloved; with you I am well pleased. Jesus was about thirty years old when he began his work. Full of the Spirit, he returned from the Jordan and was led by the Spirit in the wilderness, where for forty days he was tempted by the devil. The devil said to him, "if you are the Son of God, command this stone to become a loaf of bread." Jesus answered him, "it is written, 'One does not live by bread alone'."

(from Luke 3:21–4:4)

Times of decision can be very difficult, particularly when the choices we have to make may affect our lives for years to come, or even for as long as we live. Such choices are the cause of much stress and anxiety.

When the events in this story took place, Jesus was thirty, a time when many of us wrestle with life changing decisions, personal and professional. Jesus was feeling called to do something. We can assume that growing in his mind was the vision he would later call the kingdom of God. This vision, perhaps the ultimate vision that has taken shape in human consciousness, would mean pursuing something tantalizing and elusive. Probably there were times of great frustration for Jesus, as the immensity of the vision refused to be pinned down in neat categories. Being human, he needed time for the vision to become clear.

He knew that, somewhat to the south, John the Baptizer was addressing crowds and baptizing many. It cannot have been easy for Jesus to decide to go and listen to John and seek baptism from him. What if John's vision of the coming society were flawed? Could Jesus risk a false start to his own career? Any approach to John, particularly accepting baptism at his hands, would have to be taken in full public view. Jesus must have spent much time in prayer for guidance, taken many walks in the hills surrounding Nazareth, and perhaps talked with a few trusted friends.

John was calling people to commit themselves to his vision. Like everyone trying to probe the future, he could not be specific. He could not point to a certain kind of society and say, "That's what I want to build." All he could say was that, if people wanted a transformed society, they would have to commit themselves to lives of integrity. We know that John addressed various kinds of people and called them to lives of integrity and self-discipline. This must have made sense to Jesus, who made the decision to go south and offer himself for baptism. It was when he finally received baptism at the hands of John that he experienced a deep sense of guidance and inner peace.

Life is full of choices. Do we want the sandwich on white, brown, or rye? What kind of salad? What kind of dressing? "Decisions. Decisions," we say with a laugh. Our laughter, however, is a tribute to the power of the word "decisions." Serious decisions—and we are faced with them every day—can cause us stress and anxiety. All of us meet demons in these wilderness times of our lives, just as Jesus did. These demons are no less demons because we call them by other names in our world. Is the choice I have just made the right one, the wise one, the one I won't regret? Such anxiety can be in very real ways a demon.

At such times, how can my Christian faith play a part in the process? I find a model in Jesus' course of action. He is convinced that God has a meaning for his life and that, if he offers himself unconditionally to that meaning, a path will be shown. However, believing that this is true in my own life does not relieve me of tough thinking about my options, any more than it did Jesus. It does not relieve me of working hard, perhaps with friends and other sources of trustworthy counsel. It does not relieve me of praying simply and sincerely that my intentions and my motives may have integrity.

Even all this cannot guarantee that I will make the right decision. No doubt, even Jesus had moments of self-doubt in the months and years following his decision. But we know that when his decision had been made, and when he acted upon it and committed himself to it, he felt a deep sense of confidence and peace. May such a sense of peace be ours.

6

TIMES OF TRANSITIONS

*In the wilderness the tempter came and said to him,
"If you are the Son of God, command these stones to
become bread." He answered, "One does not live by
bread alone. . . ." The devil took him to the holy city
and placed him on a pinnacle of the temple, saying
to him, "If you are the Son of God, throw yourself
down. . . ." Jesus said, "Do not tempt the Lord your
God." The devil took him to a very high mountain and
showed him all the kingdoms of the world . . . and he
said to him, "All these I will give you if you will fall
down and worship me" Jesus said, "Away with you,
Satan!"*

(from Matthew 4:1–10)

Transition times in life can test our self confidence.
Unknown roads lie before us, and we must choose among
them. Questions press themselves upon us: "Where does
each of these roads lead? Should I choose this road rather
than another? What will the journey require of me?" And
most unsettling of all, "If I do set out on such and such
road, do I have what it takes to journey along it to the
end?"

Jesus is trying to discern how to do what he feels
called to do. He feels called by God to a public ministry.
He knows that in order to carry out this ministry effec-

tively, he must offer a clear vision to people. He wrestles within himself, as any of us would, asking questions such as, "Who am I, and who am I to be? What course am I to follow? What does God wish to use me for? What factors must I take into account, as I contemplate a certain course of action?"

The demon arrives when Jesus is at a point of very low resistance. He has been alone for some time, and he has been fasting—which means he is unusually vulnerable. In our own lives we know only too well how we can be severely tested when we are at our most vulnerable, when our spirits are low, our strength waning. Often these times are brought on by nothing more than sheer exhaustion. When our energy is low, the demons can have their way with us more easily. Often enough, the weapon we need to combat them is nothing more than plain, ordinary rest—rest that restores both body and mind to clear seeing and alertness.

The temptations of Jesus are really a succession of invitations for him to try bribing people, to dominate or impress them, and to every one of them Jesus says a resounding "No!" But perhaps the most significant thing about them is that they are all the same. They sound a little different. They occur in different locations. But all have in common an invitation to Jesus to go it alone—to carry out his mission by using power to control people instead of working together with them.

There are moments when all of us ask ourselves, "Who or what am I to become? What does God want me to be?" Most of us ask this in our early years, but for many of us the question keeps repeating itself throughout our lives. Perhaps the frantic pace of modern life and the speed with which things change causes us to ask it more often than previous generations have done. And each time we ask it, the inner wrestling can bring us face to face with the demons of anxiety and self doubt. We wouldn't be human if we did not first look for some cost-free way, the tempting way that gives us instant power.

Jesus made his choice: he walked away from the power. Having turned down the invitations to pursue his vision by his own efforts and with power over others, he walked out of the desert with his integrity in tact, headed north for Galilee, and began to call a circle of ordinary people around him. These would be his companions. These would share his vision of the kingdom of God.

At its truest, life is not a solitary journey. There may be times when it seems so, but no matter how strong or gifted we feel ourselves to be, we will serve God best if we allow ourselves the fellowship of others. To do so enriches us beyond measure. We discover, often to our astonishment, that some around us possess gifts far beyond our expectations. Even more wonderful, we find—again to our surprise—that when others participate in our lives, they draw from us gifts and insights and abilities we never dreamed we had. To go it alone, to dominate by power, is to deprive others of our gifts and to deprive ourselves of theirs. By working in community both they and we are made richer, and the sum total of power, working with God for the good of the world, is increased.

7

ENTERING INTO RELATIONSHIP

John the Baptist was standing with two of his disciples, and as he watched Jesus walk by, he exclaimed, "Look, here is the Lamb of God!" The two disciples heard him say this, and they followed Jesus. When Jesus turned and saw them following, he said to them, "What are you looking for?" They said to him Rabbi (which means Teacher), "Where are you staying?" He said to them, "Come and see." They came and saw where he was staying, and they remained with him that day. It was about four o'clock in the afternoon.

(John 1.35–39)

All of us recall moments when another person invited us into their life and into a relationship that we have treasured ever since. The other person may have been a childhood friend who has remained a friend for life, or a colleague at work, or a life partner. The significant thing is that we value the relationship beyond words. Jesus' disciples had this experience when he invited them to enter his life, probably in ways unique to each.

Here we see it happen for two of them. They are with John the Baptizer as his movement is winding down. They and he may very well be discussing, probably sadly, the decline of this great movement, wondering why it is declining and asking where God is in this. As they

converse, Jesus passes by. It is a measure of John's greatness that he points them to Jesus, unselfishly and coura-
geously. Whether they follow his suggestion immediately,
we don't know, but at some stage they take their leave of
John and set out after Jesus, probably a little wary
because they don't know him, perhaps even a little embar-
rassed, wondering how all this is going to go. Suddenly
Jesus turns around, looks at them, and asks a simple dis-
arming question: "What are you looking for?"

I like to think they were thrown by the question. It
isn't an easy question to answer! Try it yourself: "What
am I really looking for in life?" It is a deep question, defy-
ing any casual off-hand answer. We can't help smiling at
their response. "Rabbi, where are you staying?" they ask,
wriggling out of an embarrassing moment. When we don't
know what to say, we blurt out the first thing that comes
to mind, then often regret it. Yet Jesus says nothing that
would further embarrass them. Instead, he takes them at
their word and issues a warm and easy invitation: "Come
and see."

It is a wonderful moment, a moment of ease, gra-
ciousness, sensitivity, and natural hospitality. In the deepest sense they are being welcomed in. A tribute to the
richness of the welcome is that they "stay all day." An even
greater tribute to the relationship that subsequently developed is that years later one of them remembers, "it was
about four o'clock in the afternoon." This is the precise
way we recall an unforgettable experience in our lives,
every nuance etched sharply on our memory.

So we have shared a moment in Jesus' life when he
changed the lives of two people for ever. The passage
speaks to us of the necessity for hospitality in our own
lives. We give a great gift to people when we are wel-
coming and ready to include them. In some cultures

hospitality is a social obligation that people take very seriously. In our lonely North American world, it's a rarer gift. But there is more in the story for us. It lies in the awkward question that Jesus asks: "What are you looking for?" How do we respond? Is success, as it's generally understood, enough for us? Are we satisfied with the relationships in our lives? Are we happy with the contributions we're making to the good of the world? More particularly, how do we respond if we hear this question as coming from Jesus himself, the one we often call Lord? "What are you looking for?" If our reply is to request further clarification or time to consider, we can expect him to say to us, "Come and see." And if we do take up this invitation, we might consider trying what nourishes any relationship—spending time in one another's presence.

We could begin to do this by setting aside even fleeting moments to become aware of this or that aspect of Jesus' life, by recalling something he said, by looking at the word portraits of him that we have been given by four gifted writers. When we include this sort of pattern in our lives we might come to see things both about ourselves and about Jesus that we may remember for the rest of our lives.

8

THE MEANING OF FAITH

Jesus went out and saw a tax collector named Levi,
sitting at the tax booth, and he said to him, "Follow
me." And he got up, left everything, and followed him.
Then Levi gave a great banquet for him in his house;
and there was a large crowd of tax collectors and oth-
ers at the table with them.

(Luke 5:27–29)

Even when we claim to be Christian, and even when we
have a sense of obligation about worshiping and practic-
ing our faith, we may still fail to realize the effect we can
have on other people. We can make a difference even in
our professional lives when we witness to the faith that
is in us, modest though our demonstrations of it may be.

Through Levi's story Luke shows us, in a single and
seemingly casual sentence, how effective such witness
can be. People who work in most government taxation
systems tend to get used to the jokes and cracks—not to
mention the grumbles and resentments—directed toward
them. In Jesus' lifetime things were different. The Roman
taxation system employed local people to collect the
taxes. Those who took the job were paid little by the
Romans and in order to make a decent living, many
charged taxpayers a commission on top of their taxes.
This practice led to unfair and even cruel taxation if the

collector was unscrupulous, and sometimes the resentment was so great that a tax collector could be in fear of his life. Naturally, by the law of averages, there would have been decent and honest men in the profession. It may be that Levi was such a man. However, to have lasted in this profession, he must have had a measure of steel in his make up. We can assume then that, when Jesus walked into the tax office where Levi was working, he was approaching a fairly hard-nosed professional who was inured to pleas, insults, and sob stories. And yet, we are told that Levi dropped everything and responded to Jesus' invitation to join him.

We can only assume that something about Jesus called to something in Levi that was longing for fulfillment. We can also assume that Jesus did not walk in to just any tax office and speak to just any official. Perhaps one or two of the friends whom Jesus had already drawn to his ministry had grown up with Levi, or had professional dealings with him, and found him a decent and thoughtful man. Quite possibly it was their suggestion that made Jesus decide to draw Levi into the circle of disciples.

We do not know whether Levi ever went back to his office, but there is no reason to assume that he did not. Many professionals discover something immensely meaningful that makes a difference in their life, something or somebody that speaks to them at a deep level and transforms their attitude to work. The experience makes it possible for them to do their job with a greater sense of meaning and satisfaction. It may well have played out this way in Levi's life. Staying with his profession did not make him any less a disciple of Jesus. If everyone who hears the call of Jesus to be a disciple simply walked away from the world, and from the work in which he or she is experienced and gifted, then society would be a great deal poorer in the gifts that God bestows to humanity.

Levi's response to Jesus shows how powerful an act of witness can be in a person's working world. Jesus of Nazareth has made a great difference in his life, so much that Levi wishes the same kind of encounter for the friends in his profession. He gives a dinner. We can assume that at some stage in the evening he explains why he has invited his guests. We can also assume that he has told them what his encounter with this rabbi has meant to him. No doubt he was given the kind of respectful hearing that people tend to give to a colleague who has proved himself in their common world.

Think of what a difference it might make if men and women, for whom Christian faith has become significant in their lives, were to find an acceptable and non-threatening way to invite others to consider Christian faith for themselves. No fervent sermons are demanded, no impassioned pleas, no embarrassing claims to some recently gained moral superiority. Only a quiet and sincere expression of what Christian faith and Christian community have meant in one's life. The result can be quite extraordinary.

·⁖9⁑·

CHOICES AFFECTING OTHERS

Now during those days Jesus went out to the mountain to pray; and he spent the night in prayer to God. And when day came he called his disciples and chose twelve of them, whom he also called apostles. . . . Simon, whom he named Peter, and his brother Andrew, and James, and John, and Philip, and Bartholomew , and Matthew, and Thomas, and James son of Alphabets, and Simon who was called the Zealot, and Judas, son of James, and Judas Iscariot, who became a traitor.
(from Luke 6:12–13)

As anyone in professional life will attest, there is a great deal of stress in personnel administration. Small wonder! We are talking about the management of people: their careers, their relationships, their lives. The more insensitively it is done, the greater the stress for those who find their lives affected. The more sensitively it is done, the greater the stress for those who have the responsibility of management.

Jesus is about to make one of the most important decisions he will ever make. He will soon choose the inner circle of his disciples. For some time he has been meeting with certain people, individually and in groups, and sharing his vision of what he calls the kingdom of God. But there still remains the decision about who will form the inner circle of his followers—the community on which the future depends. We can assume that he feels all the anxiety that we do when we are faced with decisions that affect other peoples' lives, especially people who have invested a great deal in their relationship with us. Jesus knows, as we do, that choices must be made. As a consequence, it will be necessary to disappoint some people deeply. The simple reality is that not everyone can be chosen.

"Now during those days he went out to the mountain to pray." We can hear the hint of a lengthy process, a going apart to wrestle with what he has to do, that lasts through the long silent hours of the night. This in itself is a measure of the intensity of his thinking. The future of his vision depends to a large extent on the choices he is about to make. Jesus places the decision before God, who for him is nothing less than an intimate and loving Father.

Morning comes, and he is ready. He has made his choices. We can be certain that he has prayed not only for those chosen but for all the others as well. We can imagine the eagerness with which they await the verdict. Are they to be part of the inner circle or not? We can never know what he said to them, but we can imagine the intense disappointment of those who learn that they are not to be included in the small circle. We can assume that he is utterly sensitive to their feelings when he announces his decision. We can imagine that he tells them why this particular circle around him must number exactly twelve if it is to symbolize the new Israel of his thinking.

Knowing what we now know about those who are selected, we can see the rich humanity of this group. We know that most will show weaknesses of some kind, that some will deeply disappoint Jesus, and that one, as the writer Luke actually mentions, will betray his trust. If anything shows Jesus' full humanity, we can see it here. Jesus' choices, like ours, depend for their success on the vagaries of human nature in those whom he has chosen. There are no simple categories such as bad and good, weak and strong, wise and foolish in this circle around Jesus. In each of them, showing now an eager and dedicated face, all these things are woven together.

Many of us have to make decisions such as Jesus did that day. We make choices that deeply affect other people's lives. The image of Jesus in extended prayer suggests that, at the very least, we should tread especially carefully when making choices that deeply affect people. A lovely line of the Irish poet W. B. Yeats says, "Tread softly because you tread on my dreams."

There are moments in our relationships with other people, more often than we realize, when we may tread on their dreams. It takes only a few moments alone for us to place before God ourselves and the people whose lives will be affected by our decisions. A simple prayer for guidance may make the difference for them of a palatable new direction instead of a bitter disappointment. And it may lift from us some of the heavy burden of stress.

⊷❧10❧⊶

SEEKING TO BE UNDERSTOOD

They were in the road going up to Jerusalem. . . . Those
who followed Jesus were afraid. He took the twelve aside
and began to tell them what was to happen to him,
saying, "We are going up to Jerusalem, and the Son of
Man will be handed over. . . . They will condemn him
to death . . . mock him . . . spit on him . . . flog him
. . . kill him; and after three days he will rise again. James
and John . . . came forward to him and said to him,
"Teacher, we want you to do for us whatever we ask you"
And he said to them, "What is it you want me to do for
you?" And they said to him, "Grant us to sit, one at your
right hand and one at your left, in your glory."

(from Mark 10:32–45)

⊷❧ ❧⊶

One of life's greatest frustrations is not being understood. When an issue is dear to your heart, or even vital
to your whole purpose, it can be especially disturbing not
to be understood. Add another level of frustration: those
who misunderstand do so in the face of your best efforts
to explain. Now add a last exasperating level—they are
the very ones you gathered around you to carry out the
purpose you have in mind.

All of us have experienced at least some of these levels of misunderstanding and frustration. In Jesus' experience, all were present. Over the period of his public
ministry he tried again and again to get his disciples to

understand what he was about, what his vision of the
kingdom of God meant, and above all, what it might cost.
Time and time again they failed to hear him. Among the
gospel writers it is Mark who sees this most clearly and
tells it most unflinchingly. Jesus does not bring up the subject in the early months. He first broaches it on a visit to
Caesarea Philippi in the north. He asks the disciples who
they think he is (Mark 8:27). Hearing their replies, especially Peter's, he takes the risk of moving their understanding one step further forward. He says that being
who he is may cost him his life. Peter absolutely refuses
to hear this.

Later, as they are moving through Galilee and he was
teaching, he speaks most categorically to them about the
inevitability of his being betrayed (Mark 9:31). Mark writes
very bluntly, "They did not understand what he was saying." Rather pathetically he adds, "And they were afraid to
ask him." Their vision is too narrow. They see someone else
trying to heal the sick (Mark 9:38). They take this person
to task and then expect credit from Jesus for reprimand-
ing a competitor. Instead they are shown their pathetic
inability to see God at work in other places and people.

A young man comes to Jesus with obvious spiritual
hunger (Mark 10:21). Jesus bids him go and sell his considerable riches and give to the poor. The young man cannot face the challenge. In response, the disciples
immediately express concern about their own hoped-for
reward for faithfulness. "Look," says Peter, probably
speaking for the rest of them, "we have left everything and
followed you!" The implication is—"What's in this for
us?" Jesus tries again. They are now on the way to
Jerusalem (Mark 10:32). He spells out in detail what will
likely happen. He softens nothing, omits nothing. It is a
most explicit description of his approaching suffering and
self-sacrifice. This time their response must have appalled

him. Two of the disciples come to him privately and ask for preferment over the others, in the days of power and glory they see coming.

Even these occasions of the disciples' obtuseness do not tell the whole story. However, there is an ironic piece of good news here for anyone reading this unrelenting failure to understand. It is best introduced in a few lines of T.S. Eliot:

> To apprehend
> the point of intersection of the timeless
> with time, is an occupation for a saint—
> no occupation either, but something given
> and taken, in a lifetime's death in love . . .

We may not all be saints, or even want to be, but we can glean insight from "the point of intersection of the timeless with time," the example of Jesus in a struggling world. Again and again, he endures and counters the disciples when they misunderstand the import of his words and actions. His love and patience are boundless. Again and again, he reiterates the teaching, provides the example. Eventually his life's work culminated in a movement that has shaped the course of history and built Western civilization as we know it.

Justifiably, we may not have the patience of Christ, or want to experience "a lifetime's death in love," but even to follow his example as far as we can, as far as we dare, can offer profound hope. To the extent that we exercise patience and love toward those whom we wish to understand us, the more they will be drawn to credit our person, and perhaps our point of view, through the power of that inestimable patience and love that we find in the life and teaching of our Lord.

ENCOUNTERS

To the extent that our style of life brings us into contact with other people, we will reap the richness and the challenge of human converse. We may encounter people who need our help, or we encounter people who help us when we are in need. We may encounter someone who shows us something about ourselves that we have never known, perhaps even did not wish to know. We may encounter someone who draws from us strengths we were unaware we had. Such encounters are infinitely varied. At least some, if not all, are encounters with Jesus. We will recognize him if we are open to the possibility of meeting him.

For many who discover the gospels, the passages that speak most vividly and immediately are those in which Jesus encounters an individual man or woman. Sometimes, as with many of our own encounters, these occur unexpectedly and unplanned. Such would have been the meeting with the blind beggar Bartimaeus who, suddenly realizing that Jesus was somewhere within shouting range of him on the outskirts of Bethany, harangues the disciples until they realize that all their efforts to silence him are useless, and they bring him to Jesus.

Very often the encounter with Jesus occurs when someone is driven to connect with him because of something going on in their lives that simply must be dealt with—now. These people seek out the rabbi whose reputation is steadily growing. Such would have been the meeting between Jesus and the chief tax official named Zacchaeus, so determined to meet Jesus that he sacrifices his dignity quite publicly. In the case of the woman who approaches Jesus when he is a guest in the house of Simon, she may feel compelled to contact him out of gratitude. Something of the same inner compulsion can be seen in the encounter between Jesus and Nicodemus. This seems to be brought about by Nicodemus' intellectual curiosity. Intrigued by this country rabbi, the powerful government official is moved to an encounter that changes the rest of his life. For the woman just outside the town of Sychar her encounter with Jesus is utterly fortuitous. She goes to the well for water and finds that she is offered a drink to satisfy a much deeper thirst than she has allowed herself to admit.

Christian faith makes a deceptively simple claim: we can encounter and be encountered by Jesus in the world of own experience. To demand explanation for this claim is self-defeating. To live as if it is true, to expect that it can be so, to intentionally seek for the encounter in the daily comings and goings of life, can be to discover life-transforming truth.

⊷11⊷

FINDING SPIRITUAL STRENGTH

Now there was a Pharisee named Nicodemus, a leader
of the Jews. He came to Jesus by night and said to him,
"Rabbi, we know that you are a teacher who has come
from God. . . . Jesus answered him, "Very truly I tell
you, no one can see the kingdom of God without being
born from above."
(from John 3:1–16)

⊷ ⊶

At the heart of a truly fulfilled and productive life, we can often detect a deep faith in the transforming reality and power of God. One of the sad paradoxes of contemporary experience is that, precisely when we need the grace that comes from a living faith, life is so crowded and demanding that any thought of faith is pushed to the margins of our awareness. Very often it is a crisis that drives us to search for faith at the margins.

The life of Nicodemus is undoubtedly crowded and demanding. He carries major responsibility in his country, at a time of considerable social tension and political instability. While his religous government has authority in the land, it has to refer constantly to the greater authority of an occupying power. Such is the position in which Nicodemus finds himself as a member of the ruling Sanhedrin. Intrigued by what he has heard of the rabbi Jesus, he arranges a meeting. Nicodemus starts the conversation by complimenting, even flattering the rabbi, who shows himself to be quite unimpressed by the great man. They begin to speak of what the rabbi calls the "kingdom of God." He describes this kingdom as something born into human life—a different way of living.

Nicodemus tries to be sarcastic but succeeds only in revealing the real subject of his quest, of which he himself may hardly be aware: "How can anyone be born after he has grown old?"

As Jesus hears the question, he must see into the depths of this brilliant and powerful man. Here is a mind full of religious insight, teeming with pious legalisms, familiar with all aspects of a national sacred tradition. It would be impossible for Nicodemus to hold such a position if he did not possessed all these things. Yet Jesus can see that he has a great inner need for something more. He can see that in Nicodemus something new was struggling to be born.

Jesus offeres Nicodemus a second image of what he meant by the kingdom of God. He reminds him of the warm wind from the desert that still blows through the city in late summer, a wind that can neither be predicted nor commanded. We have no record of Nicodemus' reply. But it is significant that Jesus gives this man, who has control over so much around him, two images of things that are uncontrollable—the experience of being born and of being windswept. Jesus seems to be inviting this powerful executive to allow faith in God to enter his life, not so that he will be robbed of control, but so that he can entrust control to the source of grace, and allow the void in his life to be filled.

In Nicodemus' case we know that the rabbi succeeds. A year or two later, when on a Friday evening a friend named Joseph of Arimathea tells him that Jesus is dead on the Roman cross, Nicodemus—at great personal risk—goes with him and helps to take Jesus' body to its resting place.

How can anyone be born after he or she has become mature, holding responsibilities, having a degree of sophistication, perhaps bearing weariness from a life style bought by sustained and successful hard work? To ask this is not to find fault with a person's achievements. Through years of effort and at considerable personal cost, one may have done much good for the world. But something may be missing at the heart of it all, something that betrays its presence only at odd moments: a holiday stroll, the funeral of a friend, a solitary hotel room, the energized idealism of a grown son or daughter. What is heard and felt at such moments may be spirit hungry, or even starved, through neglect.

So how can anyone be born after he or she has become mature? For each of us the answer is a little different, but a look around reveals many people whose lives are suddenly energized or take new directions. They must have received food for the spirit, the bread of life. Those who call themselves Christian will see in this an encounter with Jesus the Christ at the heart of their own lives. And as with Nicodemus, the time spent in arranging this encounter, in preparing to meet with God, will make all the difference. The result of this encounter will be a new faith, a new conviction, a new spiritual strength.

—═12═—

ACCEPTING PERSONAL
RESPONSIBILITY

*Jesus had to go through Samaria. So he came to a
Samaritan city called Sychar . . . Jacob's well was
there, and Jesus, tired out by his journey, was sitting
by the well. It was about noon. A Samaritan woman
came to draw water, and Jesus said to her, "Give me
a drink." His disciples had gone to the city to buy
food. The woman said to him, "How is it that you a
Jew ask a drink of me a woman of Samaria?" Jesus
answered her, "If you knew the gift of God, and who
it is that is saying to you, 'Give me a drink', you would
have asked him, and he would have given you living
water." The woman said to him, "Sir, you have no
bucket and the well is deep. Where do you get that
living water."*

(from John 4:1–42)

—═   ═—

Sometimes our life may seem like a kind of citadel that
has come under sudden and fearful attack. Someone may
have challenged us. Another may have seen through the
defenses we have so carefully erected. Even the suspicion
of aggression or resistance can make us react in ways we
have long practiced, often without knowing it. Some of
us may respond with considered caution. Others may

attack the perceived invader. Still others may make an excuse and flee the encounter.

Here we are listening to Jesus speaking with a woman whom he happens to meet as he heads north to Galilee. To walk the road along the high central spine of this country is a tiring slog. In Jesus' day Jewish travelers tended to avoid this region because of centuries of ethnic hatred between Jews and Samaritans. It is about noon, and the sun is blazing down on weary travelers. Jesus is with a group of his disciples. They have just arrived at a well that has been known for millennia. Popular memory calls it Jacob's Well, because the patriarch Jacob probably brought his caravans here more than twelve centuries before.

The disciples see that Jesus is near exhaustion. They must be used to noticing the signs during these hectic days of his public ministry. They insist that he stay by the well while they go into the nearby town to get some food. Grateful for the silence and privacy, Jesus dozes in the comparative cool of the shelter around the well.

He wakes instinctively to the sound of someone preparing to draw water. He looks up, sees a solitary woman, and waits, perhaps until the first bucket is drawn. Then quietly, so as not to startle her, he asks for a drink. In this moment more than one strong taboo is broken. Men do not address solitary women, nor do Jews talk to Samaritans. With his simple request, Jesus has shattered tradition. This in itself has signaled to the woman that no ordinary encounter is taking place.

From the moment the conversation begins, there is a kind of electricity between the two. Very quickly Jesus allows the woman to recognize that he is more than an ordinary person. Although he has asked for water to drink, he says that he can give living water that will bring her eternal life. She is interested, but either she does not understand the implications or she wants to avoid them.

Then Jesus asks her to call her husband, knowing that she already has had five husbands and now is living with yet another man. He is probing her life, making her see herself as she really is, refusing to allow her off the hook. Sometimes she challenges what he says, sometimes she avoids it, leading the conversation down other avenues, especially on the subject of the differences between Samaritans and Jews. Jesus never bullies her, but he does not allow himself to be distracted. He quietly accepts her all her devices, until she tries to lead the conversation into the safe area of the Messiah's coming. Quietly and deliberately Jesus says to her, "I am he, the one who is speaking to you." At this dramatic moment the disciples return.

This conversation, the most detailed and extended in the four gospels, is a portrait of the way God deals with us. We can try avoidance, but it eventually proves impossible to sustain. Then we can move to belligerence, until its hollowness becomes obvious even to ourselves. Then we can try playing games, pretending that there are other issues at stake. One by one God deals with these devices, until we look into the mirror that God holds.

Then and there we see our true selves, the selves that God sees. And in this moment we recognize that it is God who has been the other partner in this probing inner conversation. Knowing that God sees us as we are, and yet accepts us, makes it possible to accept responsibility for our lives.

⊸⊜13⊜⊷

GIVING AND RECEIVING
FRIENDSHIP

Now as they went on their way, he entered a certain village, where a woman named Martha welcomed him into her home. She had a sister named Mary who sat at the Lord's feet and listened to what he was saying.

(from Luke 10: 38–42)

(There came a time) when a certain man was ill, Lazarus of Bethany, the village of Mary and her sister Martha. Mary was the one who anointed the Lord with perfume and wiped his feet with her hair; her brother Lazarus was ill. So the sisters sent a message to Jesus.

(from John 11:1–44)

⊸⊜ ⊜⊷

It is a pleasant occupation to call up a picture of the many friends and acquaintances who share, or have shared, our lives—family and old friends, more recent friends, acquaintances of many kinds, people we work with, people we worship with, and so on. Among the old friends we may notice two categories: those whom we have chosen and called into our lives, and those who have called us into theirs.

We speak readily of Jesus calling people. But there were also people who called Jesus into their lives. Later they may have realized that, in calling on Jesus, they had been called in return to much more than they could have imagined. Such a person is Martha of Bethany. She lived with her brother Lazarus and her sister Mary. In their culture it is unusual that none of them was married, and we do not know the reason why. They lived in the village of Bethany, today the busy Jerusalem suburb of El Azaria. Anyone coming from Jericho had to climb the long dusty road that led past Martha's house. One day, a Galilean teacher and a few of his followers came up this road. Martha happened to be outside. Something about the traveler made her issue an invitation; and soon, for the first time, Jesus was sitting in the house that would become his home away from home in the following months.

These three would become his friends, their lives intertwined in a way that would be very precious to Jesus. In this house he could relax, unwind, let go the stress of teaching and leading. There would come a day when, following Lazarus's death, Jesus would challenge death itself in this house. Meanwhile, it would be a refuge from the never ending pressure of those who were coming to regard him as subversive and dangerous.

Years later John the Evangelist would write of the day when Jesus, temporarily lying low because of a warning that Herod was ready to pounce, received the news that Lazarus was ill. John tells us with apparent surprise that, "though Jesus loved Martha and her sister, he stayed two days longer in the place where he was." Two days later the news came that Lazarus was now dead. It seems as if Jesus knew that he was being drawn to a confrontation with death itself. When he did arrive, he faced the undisguised anger and disappointment of the sisters, who felt that he had neglected them in their need. It is one of the few occasions when we see Jesus weep publicly, a measure of the deep bond formed with this family.

When we are drawn into the lives of other people and given the gift of their friendship, they in turn expect something from us. We may not realize for a long time how much we mean to them and how much they may demand of us. They may ask what we are unwilling or unable to give, and their disappointment can turn to anger and hurt, emotions that may take us totally unawares. All of this is particularly true of people in any of the so-called helping professions, but it can be true in any relationship. When we accept an offer of friendship, we must make room and time in our lives to respond as the other wishes, or at least to define the relationship in a way that will not lead to disappointment.

However, the story ends with Jesus calling Lazarus from death into life. This same Jesus had already taught that the greatest gift of love that we can give is to lay down our life for a friend. This he would do, not only for Martha, Mary, and Lazarus, but for us as well. And when God called him back into life, what extraordinary thoughts and feelings must have filled that friendly house in Bethany, as they remembered Jesus earlier challenging of death! Their new certainty is ours too. In all friendships we give our lives for others, and in turn we receive the assurance that love overcomes even death.

⟶14⟸

KNOWING STRENGTH AND
WEAKNESS

*One of the Pharisees asked Jesus to eat with him, and
he went into the Pharisee's house and took his place at
the table. And a woman in the city, who was a sinner,
having learned that he was eating in the Pharisee's
house brought an alabaster jar of ointment. She stood
behind him at his feet, weeping, and began to bathe
his feet with her tears and to dry them with her hair.*
(Luke 7:36–50)

The balance of weakness and strength in human nature
is complex and always full of surprises. The person we have
always thought strong shows an unexpected weakness.
The person we had dismissed as weak shows a surprising
strength. There seems no way of telling, except perhaps
to assume that all of us, strong or weak, are wounded in
some way, whether that woundedness shows or not.

There is a pattern among those people to whom Jesus
seems attracted and of whom he seems protective. They
have all faced some weakness in themselves, they have no
illusions about who and what they are, yet they struggle
on with their lives. Perhaps more than in any other incident, we see this played out in the house of Simon the
Pharisee. For some reason Simon, an affluent man, has

invited Jesus to a supper he is giving. The Greek word that Luke the evangelist uses for this meal tells us that it was served in the Roman manner—couches around a central open area, the guests reclining and being served. It is helpful to know this to understand what subsequently happens.

At such a meal it was customary for the poor of society to wait behind the couches until there was an opportunity to approach a guest from behind. Somewhere back in the shadows waits a woman who owes some debt of gratitude to Jesus—it may well be for healing. Seeing her opportunity, she approaches him. She has brought with her a jar of extremely costly ointment, a measure of the intensity of her feelings. She knows that, when trying to address him, she may break down emotionally. Unable to speak, she instinctively touches his feet and begins to pour out the ointment. The intimacy of touch brings a flood of pent up tears. Her head bows to hide her emotions. Years later, in language beautiful and gentle, Luke will write that she bathed his feet with her tears and dried them with her hair.

It would appear that this woman had a reputation in the community. Simon is aware of this, and he is appalled at her presence in his house. In spite of Jesus being his guest, he makes a cutting remark about Jesus' seeming ignorance of her life. Jesus does not give an inch of ground. The passage suggests a cool calm in Jesus, his words carefully chosen for maximum effect. He moves into story mode and tells of two people who are forgiven debts by a creditor. He then asks Simon a simple question: "If two people are forgiven two debts, which one will be more grateful?" Simon, a man of affairs, answers, "the one for whom the greater debt has been canceled."

Jesus compliments Simon on his correct reply. Then, turning to the woman while he speaks, he observes the lack of good manners that Simon has shown in receiving Jesus, his guest. Simon has omitted, intentionally it would seem, all the normal polite gestures one makes toward a guest being welcomed to a house. Jesus contrasts Simon's contemptuous treatment of him with the woman's grateful approach. Jesus ends with an observation about human character. This woman has no illusions about herself. She knows her own weaknesses. She knows she has great need of forgiveness. This forgiveness she has found in her encounter with Jesus. In return, her gratitude has flooded out in affection for him.

Very few of us will not have experienced joy in realizing that a harm or hurt we have done in the past has been forgiven. We taste the same joy when we know that a damaged relationship has been repaired, especially if reparation comes in the form of a generous action by the person we have hurt or wronged.

In the moment of our joy there opens another reality. We are helped to acknowledge who we really are— people capable of hurting others. We are enabled to shed illusions about ourselves. The joy of our being forgiven makes it possible to bear this awareness. The two precious gifts of forgiveness and self-knowledge are given together in a single moment, inseparable from one another.

VISION

Many things get done in the world because someone had a vision of something better. An invention provides a tool that transforms our experience. A program enhances the life of a community. A friendship encourages the achieving of a mutually agreed goal. Some visions are born of love, like a parent's vision for the future of a child. Some are born out of a searing sense of wrong and a determination to enact change, such as the cause of social and environmental justice. The wonderful thing about a vision is that the mere fact of possessing it feeds the determination to achieve its fulfillment.

Even from a quick reading of the gospels, it is obvious that the driving force of Jesus' ministry was the vision that he called the kingdom of heaven. It is quite impossible to give a neat definition of this vision. We can only begin to grasp it when we listen to the many ways in which Jesus expressed it. When asked to describe the kingdom, Jesus would reach for a simile of some sort. For him, the kingdom was always "like" something, the "like" always referring to some aspect of everyday life. The kingdom is like a tiny seed that grows; it is like a net drawn up heaving with fish.

At other times Jesus would develop an image at greater length. The kingdom is like a precious stone. Someone desires it more than anything else in the world, and will pay anything for it. Again, the kingdom is like a field in which a treasure is buried. Someone realizes this, and will give everything to purchase it. Most frequently Jesus' images of the kingdom compare it to something that we feel to be missing from our lives, and that we are drawn to search for. Finding it, we are overjoyed, and we celebrate with others. What has been lost could be a coin valued for sentimental reasons, a sheep separated from the flock, even a child who has left home.

All of these images and stories have something in common: they challenge our usual way of seeing and evaluating what we assume is reality. Jesus is offering us a new way of understanding all human experience. In this new way we realize, often with a shock, that our values and standards are radically challenged and changed. What we assume is richness turns out to be poverty, strength turns out to be weakness, and wisdom turns out to be foolishness. True riches, true strength, and true wisdom are quite other. The kingdom is a vision of a world where God reigns.

⤳15⟵

SEEING THROUGH
APPEARANCES

Jesus said "You have heard that it was said to those of ancient times, 'You shall not murder; and whoever murders shall be liable to judgment.' But I say to you that if you are angry with a brother or sister, you will be liable to judgment, and if you insult a brother or sister you will be liable . . . and if you say 'You fool,' you will be liable."

(Matthew 5:21–22)

Someone in the crowd said to Jesus, "Teacher, tell my brother to divide the family inheritance with me." But Jesus said to him, "Friend , who set me to be a judge and divider over you. . . . Take care! Be on your guard against . . . greed.

(Luke 12:13–15)

⤳ ⟵

One of our minor temptations—though its consequences can sometimes be major in our relationships—is to make judgments about people by what we see and hear on the surface. Someone responds to us with an angry word, and we assume immediately that we are the object of the anger. Someone offers compliments that flatter us, and we assume that they are genuine in their estimate of us. Someone asks for our help with a problem, and we fall into the trap of assuming that the problem as stated is the real issue. John the Evangelist wrote that Jesus "knew what was in everyone." He saw through appearances and understood immediately what the real motivations or issues were. We have just read about two moments in Jesus' ministry when he revealed this gift very clearly.

Jesus lived in a culture where the externals of speech and behavior counted for a lot. Perhaps the social purpose was to smooth relationships with ritual, to prevent problematic motivations from surfacing. Many times we hear him probe beyond these externals to reveal the reality within, the words left unspoken, the motivation sometimes not realized by the person involved.

In the first brief passage above, we are listening to Jesus address a public gathering. He quotes a law prescribing the consequences of murder. But he takes his listeners back beyond the obviously evil action. He suggests that, leading to the action, there may have been a slow growing anger, perhaps not even realized. Jesus makes a list of certain behaviors—anger, insult, contempt—and exposes their grounding in an anger that may not be realized, even if it is displayed.

In the second passage too, we are hearing Jesus address a gathering. As usual there are responses from the crowd. Someone decides that this is a chance to get some free legal assistance. Would the rabbi intervene in a family disagreement about an estate matter? Jesus refuses to be involved, but he gives a warning that takes the seemingly innocuous issue to another level: the motivation leading to the speaker's request. Jesus has moved from the surface to the depths, from the expression to the resentment or acquisitiveness that remains unexpressed. There, he suggests, lies the issue that really needs to be dealt with. These moments in Jesus' ministry are only two examples of his way of directing people to the real issue. Each time he does so, he transforms the situation by bringing people to realize that the issue is not what they think, but what lies deep within themselves.

Two of his disciples come to him and ask for prominent places in his kingdom, when he becomes politically powerful. He points out that they have not understood what he has been saying about authority—authority comes from servanthood rather than power. Later, the apostle Peter is speaking with Jesus when the younger and more intuitive John approaches, making Peter nervous and insecure. Jesus suggests to Peter that he refrain from measuring himself by the yardstick of others. In both cases, the solution to what others suppose is the problem lies in redefining it as an inner problem.

In one of W.B Yeats' plays a characters says, "The Light of Lights [God] looks always on the motive, not the deed." This is what Jesus did. When we face our own anger—our disputes and frustrations and disappointments with others—the solution may well lie within ourselves. Instead of pressing forward with our agenda, perhaps we need to acknowledge our motivations. What we see may lead us to seek forgiveness or healing.

Why am I angry? Why am I fearful? Why am I mistrustful or resentful or cynical? Even to ask the question is to begin the journey to freedom from such things.

—16—

DEVELOPING INNER SECURITY

Jesus said, "Two men went up to the temple to pray, one a Pharisee and the other a publican. The Pharisee prayed thus 'God I thank you that I am not like other people. . . .' The publican was beating his breast and saying 'God, be merciful to me a sinner.'"

(Luke 18:9–14)

(They) brought a woman who had been caught in adultery. . . . Jesus said to them, "Let anyone among you who is without sin throw the first stone at her."

(John 8:3–11)

Peter turned and saw the disciple whom Jesus loved following them. . . . When Peter saw him he said to Jesus, "Lord, what about him?" Jesus said to him, "If it is my will that he remain until I come, what is that to you? Follow me!"

(John 21:1–23)

A feature of our humanity is insecurity. We find it difficult not to compare ourselves to others. When we do so, and perceive another to be in some sense less than ourselves, our fragile ego is sometimes bolstered. However, when we perceive the other as having gifts, strengths, and abilities we do not have, our self-image is rendered inferior, or even threatened and undermined.

This episode of two men in the temple is a parable. It has the ring of actuality about it. The Pharisee is boastful and disgustingly self-satisfied. He builds self-esteem by comparing himself with someone whom he dismisses with contempt. The publican is very much the opposite. He is as aware of his unworthiness as the Pharisee is aware of his own self-defined virtue. Writing his gospel years later, Luke is quite clear about why Jesus told this parable. Around him was a circle of people who too often practiced this same contemptuous dismissal of others.

We see the same self-satisfied virtue on a second occasion, when a group of men—some scribes, some Pharisees—bring before Jesus a woman who, they claim, has been caught in adultery. John tells us that "they made her stand before all of them." One can almost feel the unctuous self-righteousness of the group. One of them further savors the moment by alleging that the unfortunate young woman was "caught in the very act." The law, they say, calls for stoning such a woman as this. Does the rabbi agree? they ask. The question is put publicly for one reason only: to trap Jesus into a statement that can be brought against him which will then make him vulnerable to the law. Jesus considers his answer carefully and clearly, doodling in the sand to give himself time. Then comes the quiet statement that cuts through the barrier of self-righteousness and hypocrisy that stands before him: "Let anyone among you who is without sin be the first to throw a stone at her." There is a frozen silence. One by one her accusers leave. Jesus keeps his eyes on the ground until all have gone. Then he and the young woman face each other.

Jesus' first word, "woman," returns her dignity. His refusal to condemn her gives her back responsibility for her own life. Her future is in her own hands. As a mature person, she is perfectly capable of making her own choices.

In the third incident, we see result of comparing ourselves with others, and finding ourselves to be inferior. Jesus has risen and is with Peter on the lakeshore. He has restored Peter to his leadership of the community. As their conversation comes to an end, the disciple John walks along the shoreline toward them. Peter shows a deep insecurity. Something in John threatens him. Perhaps it is John's confident faith, or his close friendship with Jesus. Peter asks Jesus for reassurance. Jesus replies by telling him that only one thing matters—his own faithfulness. Comparing himself with someone else is pointless and self-defeating.

We have seen two moments when people use others to shore up their own insecure self-righteousness, and we have seen a third moment when Peter is made insecure by comparing himself with another. Jesus warns us against both false assumptions. He condemns the dismissal of someone else as inferior to us. And, in Peter's case, he exposes the futility of comparing ourselves with another.

Jesus is encouraging us to develop an inner security that is neither based on contemptuously dismissing others, nor open to being threatened by the gifts of others. Jesus asks that we look for self-knowledge and self-identity in a relationship with himself. We are accepted by him, unconditionally. Our gifts are affirmed and our weaknesses known. Our whole being is understood, accepted, and loved.

⇒17⇐

THE GIFT OF SERVICE

An argument arose among them as to which one of them was the greatest. But Jesus, aware of their inner thoughts, took a little child and put it by his side, and said to them . . ."the least among all of you is the greatest."

(Luke 9:46–48)

They were on the road going up to Jerusalem, and Jesus was walking ahead of them. . . . He took the twelve aside and again and began to tell them what was to happen to him. . . . James and John came forward and said to him., "Grant us to sit, one at your right hand and one at your left, in your glory."

(Mark 10:32–45)

When the hour came he took his place at the table and the apostles with him. . . . A dispute arose among them as to which one of them was to be regarded as the greatest.

(Luke 22:14–27)

⇒ ⇐

An old seventeenth-century hymn tells us that "Pride of man and earthly glory . . . fall to dust." A twentieth-century hymn has us singing, "All that kills abundant living / let it from the earth be banned: / pride of status, race or schooling." Both hymns bid us to lay aside anything that would tempt us to "lord it over" others. Both hymns provide a difficult assignment! We are inveterate status seekers, as a vast advertising industry knows well. Our status-seeking may be followed by guilt, but before long we're at it again—a little glow of satisfaction about the make of car we drive, the area of town we live in, the name of the rather exclusive school we attended. Of course, we are not so crude as actually to boast; we merely feel our superior status with a small glow of satisfaction.

Again and again Jesus detected this status seeking in his disciples and fought against it. Is it irreverent to say that he failed? Presumably, each time he named the problem, heads would hang in embarrassment and even shame, but in time the jockeying for position would return. Human nature will win out.

There are at least three occasions, all of them in the scriptures above, when this jockeying for position shows very obviously. The first incident suggests that they have already had their argument, probably out of earshot of Jesus (or at least thinking themselves to be out of earshot). But as they gather again with him, the issue still festers, showing in their faces and body language. Jesus senses this instantly. He turns and picks up a child. Holding the child before him, he speaks to the surrounding crowd, ending his statement with the words, "The least among all of you is the greatest."

The second incident occurs near the end of Jesus' ministry. He is traveling south to Jerusalem, aware that he will most probably not get out of the city alive. Not for the first time he tries get the disciples to understand what is at stake and what may happen. He has failed in this before, and now he fails again. For they walk on. Perhaps a few hours later, and probably apart from the others, James and John ask for favors and preferment in a way that shows they have not heard a word Jesus has said. It is obviously a trying moment for our Lord.

The third incident occurs within minutes of their being seated for the last meal he is to share with them, an unfortunate timing that must have wounded him deeply. Perhaps the resurfacing of this exasperating argument is the reason why he eventually gets up from the table, takes the water container and the cloth from the door, and kneels in front of each of them to wash their feet. Embodying servanthood of the lowest kind, he pleads with them to remember that the highest calling of all is that of servant. The disciples are the heart of the Christian community. Yet even among them, we see how stubborn and resistant is the virus of pride and the desire for status. There is no magic potion for this infection. It may be the most virulent virus in our make up.

Perhaps our wisest course is to acknowledge the problem, to guard against it as best we can, and, when we realize that once again we have given in to its temptation, to ask sincerely for forgiveness and an opportunity to serve. The Lord, who did not regard his high calling as something to be exploited, took the form of a servant, and gently teaches us to be servants of one another.

⟿18⟾

CHALLENGING OUR
ASSUMPTIONS

*People were bringing even infants to him that he might
touch them; and when the disciples saw it they sternly
ordered them not to do it. But Jesus called to them and
said, "Let the little children come to me, and do not
stop them; for it is to such as these that the kingdom
of God belongs. Truly I tell you, whoever does not
receive the kingdom of God as a little child will never
enter it."*

(Luke 18:15–17)

Realizing that we have been utterly wrong about something, or about somebody, can give us quite a shock.
Realizing that the assumptions and values by which we
make our judgments are themselves wrong can be even
more unsettling. When we read the gospels with attention, we find that our Lord is constantly bringing us to
these uncomfortable realizations.

Jesus referred time and again to what he called "the
kingdom of God" or "the kingdom of heaven." He spoke
of it more often than of anything else, as if he wanted us
to share a dream or vision he had. He always spoke of
the kingdom in vivid images or stories, and these stories,
called parables, were always grounded in the ordinary

everyday things of life. The kingdom, he would suggest, is like a person who sows grain in a field. Some grows and some does not. It is like a person who loses something, searches for it, finds it, and celebrates. It is like a treasure hidden in a field, and suddenly uncovered. It is like a person who invites friends to dinner, only to find that none of them appreciates the invitation. It is like a tiny seed that grows into a huge plant.

Again and again Jesus chooses examples from everyday life to communicate his vision of life transformed. We can see a pattern in all these images and stories about the kingdom of God. All of them challenge the assumptions that we take for granted. The more examples of the kingdom we read, the more we see that what we think is primary turns out to be secondary with God. What we think shows strength is actually exhibiting weakness. What we think admirable appears as foolishness by the standards of God. What we think of as first, perhaps in importance or value, turns out to be last in God's eyes. Although on the surface Jesus' parables seem to be a collection of simple stories a child can understand, they are anything but simple. They are full of meaning that is on a collision course with our view of reality.

One day, abandoning for a moment the telling of stories, Jesus made a dramatic gesture to describe the kingdom of God. He put a child on his knee and said, "Whoever does not receive the kingdom of God as a little child will never enter it." What an affront to people who think of themselves as mature, experienced, well educated, accomplished, capable to say that a mere child is better placed than they to enter God's kingdom! What kind of kingdom is this? Surely Jesus is not saying that we can enter his kingdom only in our childhood years. He must be saying that in childhood there is a wisdom that we run the risk of losing in adulthood. A child has very little power; instead, in its dependence a child is full of trust. Life tends to crush trust as time goes by. A child is lacking in experience; instead, everything seems possible. Adulthood sadly acknowledges that some things will never be possible. A child puts no limits on love; in innocence, a child loves unconditionally. Most of our adult loves impose conditions, even if only to require that our love be returned.

Was Jesus saying that the kingdom is open only to those who embrace powerlessness and offer trust? Only to those who continue all their lives to see possibilities in seemingly impossible situations? Only to those who, despite disappointment, continue to love unconditionally? Can these qualities of childhood be retained through life or found again in our later years?

These three aspects of childhood could be called faith, hope, and love. These are the qualities in our lives that bring us into the presence of God. It is faith that ultimately brings us through darkness and doubt to knowledge and understanding. It is hope that sustains us through hard trials. It is love that, as we say, makes the world go round. To pause in the middle of our busy lives, to see through our preoccupations and accomplishments, and to reconnect with faith, hope, and love—in this way we meet the deep reality that lies at the heart of our own being, the reality that has the power to transform our lives and the lives of those around us. That is the reality we call Christ.

—✒19✑—

GIVING THE GIFT OF HOPE

*When John heard in prison what the Messiah was
doing, he sent word by his disciples and said to him,
Are you the one who is to come, or are we to wait for
another?" Jesus answered them, "Go and tell John
what you hear and see: the blind receive their sight,
the lame walk, the lepers are cleansed, the deaf hear,
the dead are raised, and the poor have good news
brought to them. And blessed is anyone who takes no
offence at me."*

(Matthew 11:1–19)

—✒ ✑—

There are moments when each of us is asked to give a
response that will make a difference in someone else's life.
Someone requests our advice. The way we reply can influ-
ence a person to take a different direction in life. A doctor must report the disquieting results of a test. How the
news is conveyed can make the difference between the
patient losing all hope or resolving to face the difficulties
ahead. A career counselor is providing guidance after a
crushing job loss. The way future options are presented
can make or break the client.

Two strangers approach Jesus and tell him that John,
his cousin and in many ways his mentor, has been put in
prison. Jesus must have been deeply distressed at the
news. Somehow John has managed to smuggle out a

message that asks an agonized question. In the months before his incarceration he became more and more certain that Jesus somehow embodied the future of God's activity in the life of Israel. Now he is beginning to doubt this. Yet he has staked everything on its being true. In his agonized doubt he sends the question, "Are you the one who is to come or do we wait for another?"

Jesus admires John very much. Immediately after he replies to these friends of John, he praises John passionately and at length: "There has arisen no one greater than John the Baptizer." It was John's impassioned preaching that drew Jesus out of private life in Nazareth and into the public ministry in which he is now deeply involved. It was John's supporting arm that held Jesus as he was immersed in baptism in the river Jordan.

Jesus must have realized the importance to John of the reply he will send. He must have known that this is possibly the last chance he will ever have of being in touch with John. He begins to frame his reply. Its content has great significance for us: "Go and tell John what you hear and see," he tells the messengers. Every element of Jesus' statement rings with a positive note. "The blind receive their sight, the lame walk, the lepers are cleansed, the deaf hear, the dead are raised, and the poor have good news brought to them." The reply ends almost on a note of defiance. "Blessed is anyone who takes no offence at me."

The reality is more ambiguous. Some were responding to Jesus; others were not. There was a great deal in the life of the people around him that was far from being changed. Death and disease continued as usual, many were blind to his ministry, many deaf to his words. Many were miserably poor and saw no hope in their lives. Yet nothing of what Jesus says is untrue. In replying as he does, Jesus chooses the evidence that will give hope to his friend at a time when hope is desperately needed.

The most wonderful gift we can give to someone is hope. This is especially important when hope is all we can give in the situation. When there has been a death, when someone lies dying, when a career is about to be cut short, when there simply is not enough money to buy what is needed—a medicine, an education, a passage away from a danger zone—these are times to speak of a situation not in terms of what it is, but in terms of what it can become. To do this is to help a person see their own circumstances from a wider or different perspective, to help them transform possible defeat into victory. Such victory may be a triumph of the heart or mind that inwardly transforms the person.

And when we find ourselves in a prison of self-doubt and anxiety, wondering whether what we have worked long and hard to achieve was worth the effort, we might consider an act of simple prayer, in which we ask our Lord to open our eyes to the worth of what we have been and what we have done.

⚯20⚯

A NEW VIEW OF REALITY

When Jesus saw the crowds, he went up the mountain; and after he sat down, his disciples came to him. Then he began to speak, and taught them, saying: Blessed are the poor in spirit, for theirs is the kingdom of heaven. Blessed are those who mourn, for they will be comforted. Blessed are the meek for they will inherit the earth. Blessed are they who hunger and thirst after righteousness, for they will be filled. Blessed are the merciful for they will receive mercy. Blessed are the pure in heart, for they will see God. Blessed are the peacemakers, for they will be called children of God.

(Matthew 5:1–16)

⚯ ⚯

All of us need continually to reexamine the assumptions we make and the values by which we live. On what basis do we evaluate other people, assigning them value and worth, or dismissing them as insignificant and unworthy? What criteria do we use to define strength, riches, ability, success? Often we hold our assumptions so deeply that we are not even aware of them. We need to hear them challenged by a voice from beyond ourselves.

The voice of Jesus challenges us in the statements that have become known as the Sermon on the Mount. In them, Jesus articulates the central vision of his earthly life, the vision he called "the kingdom of God" or sometimes "the kingdom of heaven." These statements seem to fly in the face of all reality, even of common sense. But Jesus is speaking of something far greater than what we call common sense. He is doing nothing less than outlining the values and standards of another realm of reality, another kind of world.

There is not a single sentence in this passage that has not been probed to the depths for undiscovered meaning. The words are deceptively simple; the levels of meaning are profound. A couple of examples must suffice here. Jesus says, "Blessed are the poor in spirit, for theirs is the kingdom of heaven." Again, he says, "Blessed are those who mourn, for they will be comforted."

To say that we are poor in spirit means that we understand this truth about ourselves. If we do, we realize that our steps on the spiritual journey have hardly begun and that there is always more journeying to do. To know one's spiritual poverty is to glimpse the infinite richness of the ultimate source of spirituality. For a Christian, this source is Jesus our Lord. John's gospel begins by saying that Jesus is the fullness of grace and truth. When I acknowledge my deep inward longing for grace and truth, I acknowledge in that moment my spiritual poverty and need. There is nothing sad or negative or self-defeating in this acknowledgment. Rather, it opens the channels through which grace and truth can flow. Such grace and truth are the source of energy with which to live life richly. In the moments when I open to this infusion of God's spirit, I am entering a kingdom other than that of my own self.

When Jesus speaks of those who mourn being comforted, he is pointing to a truth that has to be lived to be understood. When we experience great loss, there are many ways we can try to deal with it. For example, we can choose to deny our loss and not allow ourselves to mourn. There are reasons for such a decision. We may be extremely angry about our loss. We may have become numb from grief without even knowing that we are numb. But our Lord is saying that, if we can bring ourselves to mourn, we will open ourselves to the possibility of experiencing resolution. It becomes possible for us to be comforted. We are enabled to inhabit a new reality—a new kingdom—where comfort becomes possible, and therefore new life.

The Sermon on the Mount challenges the very way we look at reality, and turns it upside down. It offers us a strange and hopeful lens to look through, then makes us realize with a shock that this is the way God views reality. We do not always live this reality. As T.S. Eliot once wrote, "Humankind cannot bear very much reality." Yet even glimpses of it make us aware that our life is lived in the midst of what Jesus calls "the kingdom of heaven."

TRANSFORMATION

To be human is to seek some element of transformation. Perhaps we long for a relationship to be transformed into something more satisfying. We may long for a transformation in the circumstances of someone we love, and if we cannot bring this about, we may experience deep unhappiness. We may long for our own health, or even aspects of our body, to be transformed, and some of us will pay great sums of money to bring this about! There are two lines of the *Rubaiyat* of Omar Khayyam that voice all this longing: "Ah fate, if thou and I could but conspire/To change this sorry scheme of things entire."

There was a mysterious moment in the ministry of Jesus that Christians usually call the Transfiguration. It took place in the presence of only a few of his disciples, and we can presume that their community's understanding of it derives from them. As we read of the event in the gospels, we get the feeling that they struggled to find ways of describing what had happened. They had climbed with Jesus to the top of a mountain. There they experienced a mysterious change in his physical presence. His form seemed to blaze with light. Two of the great figures of Jewish history and faith seemed to be speaking with him. The disciples were shaken to the core.

This same word "transfiguration" might well be used to describe other events in the New Testament. Jesus possessed an extraordinary power to transfigure what he came into contact with. The tax collector Zacchaeus, is transfigured in a fleeting evening's visit with Jesus. Later Saul, the cruel persecutor of Christian believers, is transfigured into the great champion of Christ. Sometimes the power to transfigure is mysteriously manifested in Jesus' dealings with natural events and objects. The wedding steward in Cana dreads the shame of the wine running out for his guests. Suddenly, to his amazement, the wine far exceeds his need or expectation. On the lake the disciples are discouraged at the poor fishing. Suddenly the nets are thrashing with more fish than can be drawn in.

The question is unavoidable: What transfiguration is possible in our own lives? How can our lives be changed beyond anything we could even have imagined?

⇒21⇐

Discovering Inner
Resources

*On the third day there was a wedding in Cana of
Galilee, and the mother of Jesus was there. Jesus and
his disciples had also been invited to the wedding.
When the wine gave out, the mother of Jesus said to
him, "They have no wine." And Jesus said to her,
"Woman, what concern is that to you and to me. My
hour has not yet come." His mother said to the servants, "Do whatever he tells you.".Jesus said to them
"Fill the jars with water," and they filled them to the
brim. . . . When the steward tasted the water that had
become wine . . . he called the bridegroom and said
to him. . . . "You have kept the good wine until now."*

(from John 2:1–5)

There is a question that comes to everyone in their most
private and thoughtful moments. It is not a question we
necessarily like. It can be phrased in various ways, but one
will serve us here: If I had to face some major event or
decision or crisis in my life that really tested me, what
inner resources could I call on?

It is very early in the public years of Jesus life. He has
decided that his vocation is to communicate his dream
of a transformed world. He calls this dream the kingdom

of God. He has already called a few friends to join him. Although they spend time conversing with him and absorbing what he has to say, this does not prevent them from getting on with the ordinary things of life. It is very difficult to simply walk away from your livelihood—in their case, busy lives as fishermen on the lake—and still eat and feed your family. Spiritual growth has to take its place along with the more mundane things in life.

One day Jesus and a few of his friends find themselves guests at a wedding in a village not far from Nazareth. It may be that his mother's attendance at the wedding depended on his willingness to ·help her get there. By now she would have been well into late middle age. At some point in the celebrations the wine supply is about to run out. Somehow Jesus' mother learns of this and mentions it to her son. She gets a rather sharp reply, but her experience tells her to let it go by. She gives us an indication of how well she knows her son when we overhear, instead of a protest, her instructions to the servants: "Do whatever he tells you." She knows he will respond.

And so he does. Some large stone jars are standing nearby. Jesus tells the servants to fill them with water and take them to the wine steward. Suddenly there is more wine than the wedding can use.

What are we to make of this extraordinary story? I suggest that we think of the wedding as life itself. Like the wedding party, life is full of people dealing with the concerns of their own lives, though for a moment celebrating an event that lies a little outside the ordinary. When the wine runs out, there will be disappointment. If the wine of life is our successes and satisfactions, our creative urge and sense of purpose, then for all sorts of reasons at some stage in every life, the wine runs out. The wine can run out of a job, a friendship, a marriage—out of any of our many enterprises. Our health may fail. Or our sense of purpose in life can be quenched by depression.

Notice that Jesus makes use of water as an instrument for bringing into being a new reality. If wine is the celebration of our life, our strengths, our gifts, then perhaps water can represent the seemingly ordinary elements of our lives that rarely excite us, but without which we could not live. Often we ignore them. They are the things we take for granted—family relationships, friendships and acquaintances, daily chores and routines, the trivial round and common task. Our Lord's action offers us the possibility that in the ordinary things of life there is the stuff of transformation. Maybe there is an aspect of a well-worn relationship that we have never nourished, a talent or gift that we have scarcely developed, a startling beauty that we see in a familiar scene. These aspects of our lives can sometimes become a kind of new wine that unexpectedly makes all the difference.

Jesus' action points us to the good news that we possess unrealized resources, hidden in the recesses of our life and personality until they are forced into consciousness by our need. And when we seek these inner resources, we can encounter the miracle of Christ in our own lives, and watch him turn the water into wine.

22

Exceeding Our Expectations

Once while Jesus was standing beside the lake of Gennesaret, and the crowd was pressing upon to hear the word of God, he saw two boats there at the shore. He got into one of the boats, the one belonging to Simon . . . Then he sat down and taught the crowd from the boat. When he had finished speaking he said to Simon, "Put out into the deep water and let down your nets for a catch.".. When they had done this, they caught so many fish that their nets were beginning to break. So they signaled their partners in the other boats to come and help them. When Simon Peter saw it, he fell down at Jesus knees, saying, "Go away from me, Lord, for I am a sinful man." Jesus said to Simon. "Do not be afraid; from now on you will be catching people."
(from Luke 5:1–10).

It's seldom comfortable to remember times when someone stretched us to the limit, or pushed us far beyond the point we wished to go. We may have resented them or their demands, but now we can look back with gratitude. We have learned that what they did was done not merely to us, but for us. It was something we would never have done for ourselves.

It is early days in Jesus' ministry. He has not yet com-
pleted the selection of his disciples. By now he has made
some friends around the lake, especially among the fishing
families that are based along the north shore. But so many
people are becoming interested in what he has to say that,
on this particular day, he needs to find some vantage point
from which he can address the crowd. He is standing at the
edge of the water, facing one of the small grassy natural
amphitheaters along the shore. In front of him the crowd
waits eagerly to hear him. He needs a little space. Looking
around him, he sees two familiar figures fixing their nets
and asks for one of their boats. It is Simon Peter who
responds. He drags the boat down to the water, waits for
Jesus to get in, then jumps in himself and nudges the boat
out a few yards. From there Jesus addresses the crowd.
When the address has ended, they disperse.

The lake is quiet. Only Jesus and Simon Peter share
the silence. Jesus breaks it by suggesting that they head
out into the deep water and try for some fish. Peter
shakes his head. He tells Jesus of the futile night they
have just spent—not a fish to be had. Then for some reason Peter changes his mind. Maybe the change is trig-
gered by something about this largely unknown
companion in the boat. They start to pull together toward
the deep area. The net goes down and they wait. Peter
may be torn between wanting some fish and also wanting to be proved right about there being none.

The net immediately fills with more fish than they can
handle. Suddenly everything is action. They yell for help.
It comes. More shouting and swearing and laughter.
Many congratulations. Fish are piled everywhere on both
small boats.

It is easy to place Jesus at the edge of this scene,
to relegate him to the one-dimensional figure of much

Christian art, to imagine him standing serenely at one end of the boat, watching benignly as Peter scrambles and sweats and swears at the bulging net, with only his own strength to handle it. Instead we can use this most human moment to become more aware of the mystery we call incarnation. Imagine the scene again. This time we see two figures, naked from the thighs down, sweat coursing down their bodies, muscles rippling as they work to save this gift from the lake that is going to make such a difference to this month's budget!

Is it possible that this moment—or some such moment as this—formed the bond between these two very different men, working together at a task, sweating and swearing and laughing together. Most of us know the bonding that can take place when something achieved together can make us friends for life.

Eventually, with its gleaming writhing pile of fish, the other boat moves toward shore. Jesus and Peter are left alone again, and once more there is silence. Jesus looks at Peter. Something happens deep inside this simple yet sensitive man. He recognizes something extraordinary in this new friend who has come into his life, and he is filled with a sense of humility

There are people in all of our lives who force us out into deeper water than we wish to go, push us to perform, help us to mature, drive us to achievements of which we did not feel capable. These people, sent into our lives by God, make us realize that we are capable of far more than we ever thought. One or more of them may be making demands on us now, uncomfortable demands, exasperating or annoying demands. These people show us who we really are, and bring us to realize that we have resources, and can make contributions, beyond our wildest dreams. In all such people we find our Lord himself, who never leaves us, but enters our lives in many guises.

⊷⊸23⊷⊶

OUR ABILITY TO CHANGE

Jesus entered Jericho and was passing through it. A man was there named Zacchaeus. He was a chief tax gatherer and was rich. He was trying to see who Jesus was, but on account of the crowd he could not, because he was short of stature. So he ran ahead and climbed a sycamore tree. . . . When Jesus came to the place he looked up and said to him, "Zacchaeus, hurry and come down; for I must stay at your house today." Zacchaeus said to the Lord "Look, half of my possessions Lord, will I give to the poor." Then Jesus said to him, "Today salvation has come to this house."

(from Luke 19:1–10)

⊷⊸ ⊷⊶

We consistently underestimate how much people are capable of change, even though we are surrounded by people in whom great, often sudden, change occurs. Too often, when we think of a particular person, and estimate their abilities and personality, we assume that they are fixed entities. We even assume that about ourselves. This story shows how wonderful mistaken these assumptions can be.

The system of taxation used by the Romans in their empire was cynically clever. Knowing that military occupation and foreign rule were themselves enough to engender hatred and resentment, the Romans decided that adding taxation to their impositions might spark revolt. So instead of collecting taxes themselves, they farmed out franchises to members of the local population, who would guarantee to pay the Romans a certain return, and who then charged taxpayers a rate above the tax in order to turn a handsome profit. We can assume that those who received such franchises already had the money and resources to enforce the collection of taxes from their fellow countrymen.

All this helps us to paint a portrait of Zacchaeus as a powerful, affluent man, the owner of a large estate, a man probably surrounded by body guards. Luke tells us that Zacchaeus was not just any tax man. He was a chief, or area, tax officer. We are dealing here with considerable power. We are also dealing with someone who must have had a very thick skin. He knew that he was cordially hated and that his life might be in danger. Quite probably, therefore, we are also looking at a very lonely man.

Zacchaeus does an extraordinary thing, and we simply don't know why. Sacrificing dignity, probably risking his life in a crowd, he demonstrates an almost desperate longing to see this man of whom he has heard, Jesus of Nazareth. For Zacchaeus to do what he did suggests that seeing Jesus had become more important than anything else in his life. But why? Could the reason lie in the contrast between himself and this preacher, of whom he must have known very little? Zacchaeus's life had been spent accumulating. Jesus seemed utterly uninterested in anything more than minimal possessions. Over the years Zacchaeus had done much injury to other lives. Jesus was known widely as one who brought healing. Zacchaeus was cordially hated. Jesus, at least at this stage in his career, was deeply loved. From Zacchaeus most eyes were averted. To Jesus most eyes turned.

In the lamp lit room with its well laid table, we witness a moment in life when suddenly many things are resolved and a great change takes place. In the mirror of Jesus' eyes across the table, Zacchaeus sees himself in a new way and is revolted by what he sees. A new man comes into being, a man whose old courage is turned to new use as he gives up much of what he is and owns, and takes on a new identity.

It is not too difficult for us to understand such a sudden change; we can recognize it from our own experience. There comes a time in life when things neglected become important, when things that have long been on the back burner suddenly demand to be moved forward. For the most part they tend to be things left undone: relationships neglected, even injured; apologies often intended, but never given; journeys dreamed of, but not yet taken; hurts done, needing to be healed - hurts to others and hurts to ourselves; talents or feelings that have never found expression; choices that made other choices impossible, and now the other choices clamor for fulfillment.

Then some event occurs, or perhaps more likely, no event occurs, and we have time for awhile by ourselves. Suddenly we begin to see ourselves as if in a mirror. And in that moment of self-reflection, who is to say that we are not seeing ourselves reflected in the eyes of Jesus? Can we, like Zacchaeus, take on the new identity that has been crying for recognition, and set off in a new way through life?

⇥24⇤

SEEING OTHERS IN A
NEW WAY

*Six days later, Jesus took with him Peter and James
and his brother John and led them up a high mountain, by themselves. And he was transfigured before
them, and his face shone like the sun, and his clothes
became dazzling white. Suddenly there appeared to
them Moses and Elijah, talking with him.*

(Matthew 17:1–9)

In almost every relationship there are moments when we
see another in a new way. We realize things about the
other person that we never expected. Sometimes this
happens because the other wishes it to happen, and we
are deliberately allowed into their lives. We can be astonished, moved, impressed, appalled, or humbled, depend-
ing on what we suddenly see in the other.

We are being shown such a moment in Jesus' relationship with a group of his disciples. We don't know precisely how long they have been with him. There have been
at least some months of listening to him, overhearing him
speak to others, gradually learning to question him,
watching him heal the sick, seeing him in every mood.
Three of them, Peter, James, and John, are about to learn
that there is yet more to be discovered about this man,

who has befriended them and called them to be partici-
pants in implementing his vision. We cannot guess why
Jesus selected them from among the twelve, nor can we
know if there were any feelings of resentment on the part
of those excluded.

Mount Tabor, one of the hills in southern Galilee, is
most likely to have been the mountain that Jesus decided
to climb with Peter, James, and John. They would never
forget what happened. Just as they found this episode difficult to describe—which they must have done many
times in the years ahead—it is difficult for us to find language that helps us to be present on the mountain. But
they must have seen Jesus in a very different light than
they had ever before seen him, different than they had
ever imagined. We often use their kind of language when
we try to describe a moment of intense, even blinding,
realization about someone.

On a clear day the disciples could see from mount
Tabor the high points of Jerusalem away to the south. This
was the power center of their world. And somehow they
began to see Jesus as a towering figure in the long story
of their faith, equal to its giants Moses and Elijah. It is
as if these men for the first time saw with blinding clar-
ity the majesty of Jesus. The theologian Helmut Thielike
believes that nothing changed in Jesus at the time, but
that the disciples were allowed for a fleeting moment to
see him as he really was—the embodiment of the glory
of God.

It is plain that Peter was particularly moved. All his
life he had known the spiritual giants of faith in imagination. Now the veil seemed to have been drawn aside,
and he had entered their world. He wanted this moment
to last. He would promise anything to keep this vision.
A shrine to mark it? Certainly! Three shrines? Yes! One

thing alone he is sure of—trust in his friend Jesus. The validation of his friend thunders in Peter's head like a great voice saying, "This is my son."

All of us have known moments of transfiguration, when some aspect of our life is radically changed. These are not necessarily merely religious moments. Very often such things begin in the ordinary and in the least expected way. The individual we have never respected displays an unexpected courage or insight that fills us with admiration. An opponent or rival who has often made life difficult for us shows such compassion that we are surprised and humbled. In a relationship that has become humdrum, something allows us to see the other person as we have never seen them before, and the relationship moves onto an entirely new footing. All of these are glimpses of the transfiguring glory of God.

We cannot prolong or hold onto these glimpses, but our relationship with the other person will never be the same again. It is as if we had heard a voice proclaiming that we are in the presence of someone who is precious to God, and have felt the power of God working through the other person to transfigure our own lives.

HEALING

One of the great changes that has taken place in Western culture during recent years has been the rediscovery of the hidden dimensions of healing. We are constantly reminded that healing is related to such terms as "whole" and "wholeness." All of us long to be whole - fully healthy in body, mind, and spirit.

We are becoming aware in medical practice that wholeness can be different from curing. Any professional knows that a person can be cured of an illness but remain broken in spirit. Such a one has been cured but not yet made whole. There are times when an illness cannot be cured but, in some wonderful way, the person can achieve a wholeness of spirit that enables them to live creatively and even joyfully. There are many means by which we can be made whole. We can be brought to wholeness by a professional using modern medicine. Wholeness can come through a loving relationship. It can come through disciplined prayer. Sometimes the bridge between brokenness and wholeness is crossed because of some grace-filled moment when something is said, some gesture is made, some insight is gained that makes all the difference.

Jesus healed frequently and in many ways. At times he touched and prayed, dealing with a physical condition such as leprosy or deafness. At times he struggled to bring about healing, as with a demented man on the east shore of the lake, or with an epileptic child brought by a beseeching parent. There were times when Jesus, human in his exhaustion or in the limitations of his own self-understanding, had to be begged to heal, as with the courageous and stubborn woman who encountered him on the Mediterranean coast. Not one of us is entirely whole. To be human is to be wounded or limited, whether the wound or limitation be physical, mental, or spiritual. We all choose different ways to find wholeness. But among them, a growing relationship with God, or membership in a Christian community, can offer resources for achieving wholeness that can sometimes astonish and overjoy us.

⟶25⟵

THE SEARCH FOR HEALING

*They brought to Jesus a deaf man who had an imped-
iment in his speech; and they begged him to lay his
hand on him. He took him aside in private away from
the crowd, and put his fingers in his ears, and he spat
and touched his tongue. Then looking up to heaven,
he sighed, and said to him "Ephphatha," that is, "Be
opened." and immediately his ears were opened, his
tongue was released, and he spoke plainly. . . . They
were astounded beyond measure, saying, "He has done
everything well, he even makes the deaf to hear and
the mute to speak.*

(from Mark 7:31–37)

⟶ ⟵

Not one of us is without an experience of some kind of
healing. We can recall the small illnesses of childhood that
usually pass in a few days and are followed by the heady
feeling of being out playing again with friends. Adult life
brings illnesses, some quickly passing, others with worrying implications. We know people who have struggled
hard for health, and we ourselves may have struggled
hard. There may have been illnesses so serious that life
itself was at stake, and yet a way was found to bring us
renewed health and quality of life. Or there may be in
our experience a condition or debilitating disease that
limits us, or someone we know, and is a heavy burden.

But even here, the support of friends and professional healers has made a great difference to the way we, or the other person, has been able to cope and bear the disease. While there has been no cure, there has been some healing.

Jesus is now on the north-west coast of the Sea of Galilee, the farthest he ever ventured from his homeland of Judea in the south. Here he encounters a person who is deaf. Because the man is also having difficulty with speech, he may have been profoundly deaf, unable to hear language and learn how to articulate clearly. At such moments in the gospels the sheer detail and vividness of the writing convince us of the authenticity of the events. Jesus' taking the man away in private, putting his fingers in his ears, spitting and touching the man's tongue, even the detail of looking up to heaven—everything speaks across time and draws us into the moment.

There is another detail, easy to let pass. Jesus sighs before he carries out this healing. Is such an apparently insignificant detail yet another indication that this gospel writer may be a doctor? If so, he would know what everyone in the healing professions knows. Healing of any kind is costly. Ask any nurse, any doctor, any counselor. Even in family life we are aware of the cost involved in healing wounded relationships, and in trying to deal with past hurts. As we hear Jesus sigh, we become even more aware of the mystery we call incarnation. For it is in this moment, when we witness the mysterious power of his healing touch, that we are also made aware of his human weariness.

Now we see the relief and hear the rejoicing. Excited and astonished friends are celebrating with this jubilant man the giving of new life. They insist on telling everyone they meet about what has happened.

We can put ourselves into the place of the one who was healed, knowing that each of us needs healing. In this case we might ask: Do I need my own ears freed of deafness I may not be aware of? Are there important things I am not really hearing? The people with whom I live and work, the people whom I love and who love me: Are there things they wish me to hear about myself, my attitudes, my words or actions, my lack of sensitivity in some aspects of life? Have my own inner voices been muted by the deafness that can come from too much busyness?

And when the Lord's fingers have touched my ears, what will I begin to hear, to realize, that previously I have missed?

Perhaps I need God to release my tongue, to free my speech so that I become capable of saying things I find difficult to say, because the words won't come or the cost of saying them feels too great. Are there people to whom I need to say that I am sorry? Are there those to whom I need to say "I forgive you" or "Will you forgive *me*?" Are there some to whom I need to say "I love you," to stop assuming that they already know? And when I feel the Lord's finger on my tongue, what gentle words will I speak to heal and be healed?

Sometimes we ask for healing, and sometimes like the deaf man in the story, we have to be brought to healing by those who wish us well. It is always available, and when it comes, we feel the touch of Jesus' hand.

-◦26◦-

THE SOURCE OF HEALING

Jesus went away to the district of Tyre and Sidon. Just then a Canaanite woman from the region came out and started shouting, "Have mercy on me, Lord, Son of David; my daughter is tormented by a demon." But he did not answer her at all. And his disciples came and urged him, saying, "Send her away, for she keeps shouting after us."

(from Matthew 15:21–28)

-◦ ◦-

All of us have discovered—sometimes to our embarrassment and sometimes to our great pleasure—that first impressions can be quite wrong, and we have been forced to revise them. We can recall those occasions when someone, whom we had instinctively dismissed as unimportant in our lives, turns out to be of great importance indeed, when they become the means of changing our lives by something they do for us or say to us.

By this stage in his ministry Jesus has become a public figure, known across Galilee as a person of wisdom and a source of healing. Wherever he goes, crowds gather and the sick are brought to him. From more than one incident in the gospels we know that healing drains him. Like us, Jesus knows he must rest. To rest he must take a holiday and get away. The question is, to where? Jesus decides to take a group of his disciples and head north-west across the province toward the Mediterranean coast. The mere fact of being away must have lifted some of the weariness and stress. We can therefore understand the reaction of the disciples when a woman of the coastal area begins to follow the group. This is the last thing they wish for their master at this moment. However, the woman will not be turned away. Her child is ill and she is desperate.

The disciples cannot get rid of this woman. They now ask Jesus himself to send her away, so that he can recover from his exertions. Probably they mean well. His welfare is their primary concern. Although Jesus does not directly dismiss the woman, he does attempt to disengage himself from involvement. "I was sent," he says, "only to the lost sheep of the house of Israel." By any interpretation the woman is excluded. She is not repelled. Once again she asks for help. This time Jesus' reply is even sharper. His reference to dogs is hurtful in any language. In reply she turns his own words back to him in a most determined and courageous fashion. "Even the dogs," she says tartly, "eat the crumbs that fall from their masters' table." The effect is extraordinary. The weary Jewish rabbi, aware mainly of his own exhaustion and his wish to be left alone, looks hard at this woman. It is as if his Jewish horizons and boundaries begin to roll back to encompass far more than the small country of his birth. His sense of vocation begins to change.

We cannot be certain, but this may be one of those moments when the true extent of Jesus' vocation begins to appear to him, calling him far beyond his own tradition and nation. We can't help thinking of the great commission that he will one day give these disciples, sending them as witnesses not only in Jerusalem, not only in Judea, but to the ends of the earth. Did this vision first begin to germinate in Jesus' mind as he looked at this woman who stood before him—needy, vulnerable, distraught with anxiety about her "beloved child"?

When we imagine a scene in which our Lord is involved, we tend, quite rightly, to see him as the source of inspiration and grace for others. But this scene is different. He is of, course, the source of healing and grace for this woman and her daughter, but before this occurs she deeply affects and even changes him. She has been the means of his growing and maturing. Through her, he has been given a vision of the greatness of his mission.

Such changes in ourselves can be brought about by people who we never expect will change our lives. The sudden remark of a child that brings us up sharply. The gentle observation of an older person, who tells us something about ourselves. The insight of someone, an employee perhaps, who is vulnerable to us, yet has the courage to mention a trait that we have never acknowledged. The words of a perceived adversary that strike home to us and make us look again at ourselves and the relationship. The tone of voice of a loved one that surprises us and makes us realize that a central relationship in our life requires some work. Or words from the same person that make us glow again with love.

In all such situations as these, the one we ignore or would dismiss becomes the source of our healing. In each encounter, we can recognize that the Christ has once again entered into our lives.

COST

In flippant phrases, such as "there is no free lunch," we acknowledge a deep truth about life. Everything has a price. We could add that the greater the thing is, the more real and true it is, the greater its cost is likely to be. This is why love can be the most costly thing of all. Here is a great mystery, for those who have gained love at great cost tell us that it was worth it, whatever the price may have been.

When we think of the cost to Jesus of the work he did, we recall the many images in Christian art that show him responding to human need. We see him healing and helping. We see him with children or disciples. But then we remember the images of dreadful suffering that he endured in the agony of Roman crucifixion. Beyond those images we see him risen, glorified, majestic.

Jesus experienced much of the stress that we do, as well as the stress that affects men and women who live public and high-profile lives. Surely Jesus felt the stress of youthful growing when, like all of us, he must have struggled with the restrictions that children and young people feel, especially parental control. Later, during the

hidden years in Nazareth, he would have wrestled with
the stress of deciding on the future course of his life,
among the many possibilities that presented themselves.
When he finally decided to leave and to offer himself for
John's baptism, there must have been stress. He was leav-
ing his family and identifying with a movement that was
at least politically suspect.

His wilderness experience was another time of decision. And forming a community of disciples must have
been difficult. The effort to make them understand his
vision of the kingdom of God was obviously frustrating.

The gospels do not hide Jesus' frequent exhaustion
from the demands made upon him, especially the work
of relieving human suffering. The presence of crowds,
always fickle, were always potentially dangerous in a
volatile society. Hostile forces gathered as his movement
gathered strength. There was the treacherous question
that could come at any moment and the growing knowledge that enemies were closing in. And finally, there was
the slow realization that his vision would demand the ultimate self-offering. All of these things constituted deep
and costly stress for Jesus.

When we list such stresses, we realize even more
clearly the degree to which his life and its experience
reflects our own. We realize, too, how much a careful
reading of the gospels speaks to our own stresses, and can
be a source of grace for us.

⟶27⟵

SURVIVING IN THE CITY

*Jerusalem, Jerusalem, the city that kills the prophets
and stones those who are sent to it! How often have
I desired to gather your children together as a hen
gathers her brood under her wings, and you were not
willing!*

(Matthew 23:37–39)

*They sent some . . . to trap Jesus in what he said. They
came and said to him, "Teacher, we know that you are
sincere, and show deference to no one . . . but teach
the way of God in accordance with. Is it lawful to give
taxes to the emperor or not?"*

(Mark 12:13–17)

⟶ ⟵

Our culture is largely urban. Most of us live in or near
cities, and even those of us who don't are connected to
them—buying the products available only in cities, visit-
ing the hospitals, watching television programs produced
there. We are familiar with the city's highways and traffic, its frustrations and dangers. We are also aware of its
resources for living, and we appreciate them. We may
grumble at rising taxes, fume in long lines, and fulminate
against city hall, but the city remains important in to lives.

Christian faith has a strange relationship with the
city. Hymns tend to speak of the earthly city with less
than complimentary images. The simplicity and purity of

the countryside—real or imagined—is seen as a more fit-
ting place for Christian life. We warm to images of small
country churches in suitably leafy surroundings, of fair
meadows and fairer woodlands, high mountains and rush-
ing streams . . . our idealized escapes from urban living.

If we observe Jesus in the city, in his case mainly
Jerusalem, we discover that he, like us, seems to have had
an ambivalent relationship with it. This is not surprising,
because Galileans never felt comfortable in Jerusalem.
There were differences of culture, history, and political
attitude. The conservatism of Jerusalem was always wary
of outsiders. But as we trace Jesus' activities in the city,
we can see a very interesting progression. As a small
child, he is brought to the city to be presented to God
at the temple. This was the custom for all newborn children, if the journey were possible for the family. Some
twelve years later he is again brought to the city, and this
time he gets separated from his family. After a frantic
interlude, he is found in the Temple area. During the
eighteen years when we have no evidence of his movements, he may have been present for some of the many
annual holy days that were kept with great pomp in
Jerusalem.

Throughout his years of public ministry he made a
number of visits there. At this stage his attitude to the city
(and its attitude toward him) becomes darkened by confrontation. We hear him passionately venting his frustration about his reception in the city. Later he actually
weeps over Jerusalem, crying out, "If you had only recog-
nized on this day the things that make for peace!" Time
goes by and things harden even more. Jesus discovers
strong and determined enmity in the city. At first it comes
in treacherous questions, like the one quoted above that
was designed to trap him and make him vulnerable to the

authorities. He has only to answer unwisely, and he is in serious trouble. This enmity grows until his opponents at last attack, and the great drama of death and resurrection begins.

The pattern of Jesus' experience with the city is not so different from our own. We too are presented to the city scene, perhaps to get an education or to seek and find a job. Even if we were born and brought up in the city, seeking employment can be a troubling exposure to urban realities. As we try to make our place at work and in social life, we may feel lost and out of our depth. Then come the challenges, some of them very tough when we are slapped down hard. There will almost certainly be times of weeping—quite possibly a literal weeping—in frustration or vulnerability or apprehension. At times there will be hurtful confrontations that will severely test our inner strength. There will almost certainly be enemies, both among our colleagues and our competitors. From time to time the nails of various professional and personal crucifixions may bite hard. Always the test will be whether to crumple up under the pressures, or to continue with the lives we have set ourselves to lead; whether to strike back in anger at those who set obstacles in our way, or to proceed circumspectly but with generosity of spirit. There is no assurance that we will achieve success as we have envisaged it.

For Jesus, even crucifixion was not the end. It gave rise to amazing new life. For us too, even the worst and hardest challenges hold out the possibility of results that we could never have imagined, results that keep both us and the city alive.

⊶28⊷

FINDING RELAXATION
AND PEACE

The apostles gathered around Jesus and told him all
that they had done and taught. He said to them,
"Come away to a deserted place, all by yourselves and
rest a while." For many were coming and going, and
they had no leisure even to eat. And they went away
in the boat to a deserted place by themselves.

(Mark 6:30–44)

⊶ ⊷

As the stress of contemporary life increases, so also does
the need for some relief from that stress. The day is long
gone when such things as retreats were encountered only
in the context of the religious life. In every kind of insti-
tution people are encouraged to set aside some time
where there is at least a change of pace in their activities. It may be nothing more than a weekend when com-
pany policy is discussed, and time is set aside for personal
reflection. Yet this happens in surroundings that engender peace and relaxation.

If Jesus of Nazareth is a significant figure in someone's life, the chances are that they will place him in the
setting of the north shore of the Sea of Galilee. This
stretch of water, about twelve miles long and four miles
wide, figures in many episodes of Jesus life. It is here that

he came to begin the three fleeting years of his public ministry.

Here, in the small fishing town of Capernaum on the stony shoreline, he walked toward two young fishermen who worked the lake for their livelihood. He chatted with them and asked them to give him some of their time. Years later they would realize that their decision to follow him had changed them—and changed the future of the world for ever.

Later he told them that there would come when they would "fish for people"—a statement that initially must have puzzled them. But eventually they would come to understand, as they saw a new movement developing around them, spreading far beyond the small world in which they had grown.

Even today an interesting feature of this northern half of the lake is the difference between the western and eastern shores. All down the western shore there is habitation and development. At night the lights shimmer on the lake, the lights of homes and institutions, the blazing lights of hotels along the lakefront in Tiberius. Sounds continually travel across the water—the hum of traffic, the snatch of music for a night club.

The eastern shore is very different. Along this upper shore, across from the ruins of Capernaum, the fishing town that Jesus called home for a few short years, there is a line of darkness pinpointed by lights at distant intervals, security lights in some industrial or military installation, lights to mark a highway intersection.

Jesus responded to the difference in these two shorelines. There is not a single reference to his having visited Tiberius, a center for play and relaxation then and now. When we consider the demands and stresses of Jesus' ministry, it is not surprising that he felt no need to seek out more crowds, more noise, more false stimulation. But we are struck by the number of times he turns to the disciples and suggests that they go over to the other side—always meaning the quiet side, the side of solitude. This is where he goes when he wishes to avoid the crowds. Sometimes even here he does not get a break. But it is where he tried to find retreat and rest.

It is hard for us in our culture to admit that we need relief from stress. To admit this need feels like weakness, and raises the fear that others may perceive us as weak. Will taking time out be seen as an admission that we cannot handle the job? Will it cut us off from consideration for promotion? Will it arouse whispers behind our back, saying we are "losing it"? So we hesitate to "go to the other side," to take time for some relaxation and refreshment.

The ability to rest is marked in the life of Jesus himself, a life we seek to emulate in our daily living. By seeking the solace of relaxation he sought, we will also discover, through him, the source of refreshment he enjoyed.

⟶29⟵

RELIEVING ANXIETY
AND STRESS

*That evening at sundown, they brought to him all who
were sick or possessed with demons. . . . He cured
many who were sick with various diseases.*

(Mark 1:29–34)

*The scribes and Pharisees brought a woman who had
been caught in the very act of committing adultery. . . .
Jesus bent down and wrote with his finger on the ground.
When they kept on questioning him, he straightened up
and said to them, "Let anyone among you who is without sin be the first to throw a stone at her.*

(from John 8:1–11)

⟶   ⟵

What name will the future give to our age. A number
of possibilities come to mind, one of which is the Age of
Stress. The word is everywhere when people are discussing their daily lives. Library shelves are bending under
the weight of books on the subject: how to avoid stress,
how to lessen stress if one is suffering from it, how to stop
worrying and *enjoy* stress—on and on the titles and the
promises go. Drug stores offer a variety of remedies for
the same complaint. Doctors' offices are full of patients
whose symptoms are frequently attributed to stress.

Yet in Christian thinking, when it comes to portraying the life of our Lord Jesus Christ, mention of stress is strangely omitted. Certainly we are aware of his great suffering. The central symbol of the faith—the cross—ensures this. But except for this last period of his life, Christian art or writing portrays little of the day to day stress of his ministry. Instead, apart from the scenes of his passion, most Christian art shows Jesus helping, teaching, blessing, healing. He appears as an unselfish resource for others, but he himself, for the most part, appears calm and serene. In reading the two moments of scripture above, it is easy to miss the underlying tension that, for Jesus, must have caused stress time and time again.

The first passage illustrates one source of stress. When he was attracting large crowds and his reputation as a healer had spread far and wide, he must have been under constant relentless pressure to respond to people's needs. Wherever he went, he was surrounded by their endless ills. All were demanding; most were deserving. To carry such expectations must have been draining. He must have been exhausted, and we are only too aware of the stress that comes with exhaustion.

The second incident imposes a different kind of stress. Although the apparent issue is the woman and her alleged crime, the real issue is something else. Here is one of the many attempts to trap Jesus into a public statement that can be challenged by rabbinical law and possibly provide an excuse for a serious charge against him. This is nothing short of an attack with a concealed weapon. The weapon is the unfortunate young woman. Here Jesus is facing deadly enemies. At least one human life is at stake (the woman's), and probably two (his as well), and there is a collision between strict moral law and the law of love.

When asked for his opinion about the punishment due the woman, Jesus responds with a statement that silences criticism and baffles would-be accusers. We might ponder the stress that Jesus was under in parrying this verbal attack and in seeking to shelter the woman from physical attack.

Such moments were frequently experienced by Jesus. The knowledge that there may be political watchdogs in a crowd, listening and noting everything we say; the expectation that at any moment a hostile question may come from a group; the growing realization—as he must have had—that someone could at any time betray us to the authorities: all these things are great sources of stress.

These days, most organizations are under stress, as well as those who work in, for, and with them. Very often, even if the Christian faith is significant for us, we hesitate to make links between what we read in the gospel and our own everyday experiences. We tend to think of the gospel as somehow part of our "religious" life, and our stresses part of our "real" life. In large measure, the problem lies in the way that the gospel is represented to us. It is not enough merely to believe that in Jesus we see God entering into our human nature. We need to realize that all aspects of our human nature are present in Jesus. If when we are stressed, we turn in simple, even momentary prayer to him, we can be certain that the one to whom we pray knows our stress.

⟿30⟾

FACING MORAL PROBLEMS

The soldiers, their officer, and the police arrested Jesus and bound him. First they took him to Annas who was the father-in-law of Caiaphas, the high priest that year. Caiaphas was the one who had advised that it was better to have one person die for the people.

(from John 18:1–24)

Pilate went out again . . . and told them, "I find no case against him. But you have a custom that I release someone for you at the Passover. Do you want me to release for you the King of the Jews? They shouted in reply, "Not this man but Barabbas!" Now Barabbas was a bandit. Then Pilate took Jesus and had him flogged.

(from John 18:28–19:16)

⟿ ⟾

Somewhere between Christian faith and professional life there lies a no-man's-land where land mines are buried, waiting to explode. The mines are moral questions that Christian faith poses for professional life.

When we meet Pontius Pilate, the representative of Roman power in Judea, we meet a flawed and compromised figure. Long before he sits to preside at the trial of Jesus, Pilate has in various ways made himself financially vulnerable to those over whom he is supposed to exercise power. Consequently, this seemingly powerful figure is really helpless. Caught with Pilate in a net of intrigue and compromise is Caiaphas the high priest. He is responsible to Pilate for keeping the peace, just as Pilate is responsible to Rome. He is trying to preserve a balance between the warring religious parties and to avoid breaches of the peace. Also, local society is resentful of Roman occupation, and always threatening to revolt, especially if there is a figure to rally around. Some think that Jesus of Nazareth is such a figure.

In the end, both of these men conspire to bring about a death that will haunt humanity far into the future. Yet by what standards do we judge them? Perhaps if we had known them at the beginning of their respective careers, we would have detected all the idealism and good intentions that are present at the beginning of any career. Yes, each was going to make a name for himself. Yes, each intended to make a difference to things, and to do so honorably. Even if we look at this low point in each man's behavior, resulting in the death of an innocent man, we can justify their actions by criteria we ourselves might use frequently in public or professional life.

There comes a point in the trial when Pilate can see that things are getting out of control. All indications in scripture point to his hoping to find a way out of the death penalty. In desperation he decides to give the crowd some satisfaction. He will have the prisoner flogged. It is a dreadful punishment, but at least it is not crucifixion. Pilate is acting in self-preservation. Who of us has not done so at some time or other?

Then consider Caiaphas and his complex responsibility. At a meeting some days before Jesus' trial, he had said it was expedient that one man should die for the people. Behind this statement there were pressures. A condition of his agreement with Pilate and Rome was that public order would be kept. No Messianic movements. No outbreaks of rebellion. If they did occur, then the tenth legion would march from Damascus to quell any disorder. This would be done efficiently and brutally, and all local governance would be withdrawn. Like Pilate, Caiaphas is being a responsible senior executive in making an agonized choice for what he sees to be the lesser of two evils.

We should think twice before joining in the judgment of these two people. The decisions they made are familiar to those who carry executive responsibility. For this industry to survive , such a such a number of people must be downsized out, laid-off, deprived, regrettably, of their livelihood. To maintain the credibility of the organization, this or that officer must be sacrificed, fired, terminated. Are we speaking of villainy or of inevitable realities in the human situation? We are speaking of the moral burden borne in some sense by all of us, that of acting in a morally complex world where there are few easy solutions and no perfect ones.

Christian faith is honored when we seek, in so far as it is possible, to act with the compassion of our Lord and with his infinite respect for the other, even at cost to ourselves. There will be times when our action must be a compromise between the demands of the situation and the needs of those involved. At such times we need to be aware of the compromises by which we survive, to ask forgiveness for weaknesses that have dictated our decisions and actions. If we seek such forgiveness, then we are forgiven. Knowing this, we can retain our hold on Christian faith in our public life.

❧31❧

RESPONDING TO SUFFERING

When they came to a place called Golgotha (which means Place of a Skull), they offered him wine to drink, mixed with gall; but when he tasted it he would not drink it. And when they crucified him, they divided his clothes among themselves by casting lots; then they sat down and kept watch over him. . . . From noon on, darkness came over the whole land until three o'clock in the afternoon. And about three o'clock Jesus cried with a loud voice, "Eli, Eli, lama sabacthani? That is, "My God, My God, why have you forsaken me?" Then Jesus cried again with a loud voice and breathed his last.

(from Matthew 27:27–61)

❧ ❧

A supreme test of our character is how we respond to our own suffering. The ways that we react are as varied as our personalities. Sometimes we are quickly overwhelmed, and surrender to the darkness that has entered our lives. Sometimes we discover resources that we never dreamed of. Far from becoming self-centered, we may receive extraordinary grace in our suffering, which enables us to reach out in loving concern to those around us. To encounter this costly grace, either in oneself or in another, is to feel oneself near to God.

The death by crucifixion of our Lord Jesus Christ is another example of extreme courage. Because Christians ascribe divinity to Jesus, we have tended to overlook the indescribable suffering of the crucifixion. We need to remember that Jesus' death involved the pain of a fully human person, that it was chosen freely, and that it had at its heart an unyielding and costly purpose. He could have retreated at any time before he gave himself to arrest and sentencing. This has never been more profoundly expressed than in the simple words of Mrs. Cecil Alexander's hymn:

> We do not know, we cannot tell
> What pains he had to bear.
> We only know it was for us
> He hung and suffered there.

The first moment of what we can only call moral majesty comes when Jesus is being fastened to the cross. He has been thrown to the ground, the long spikes smashed into his wrists and anklebones. He is then hoisted aloft as the cross crashes into its retaining hole. At some moment this prisoner is heard to say, "Father, forgive them, for they know not what they do." We will never know who heard that prayer gasped out in excruciating pain.

In the dreadful cry that he makes only minutes before he dies, there was a mental agony we can only try to imagine. He had always felt and spoken of an intimate relationship with God, so intimate that he constantly used the word *Abba* to describe it, a term that points to the utter trust of a child in a loving parent who will never betray such trust. Now, almost demented by physical pain, probably moving in and out of consciousness, he is afflicted by the terrible thought that his trust has been betrayed. He is utterly alone.

Matthew the evangelist tells us that Jesus cried out again just before dying, but he does not tell us what Jesus said. It is Luke the evangelist who tells us that Jesus roused himself for a final moment to call out, "Father, into your hands I commend my spirit." It would seem that Jesus had recovered from a sense of betrayal and now, despite the pain and fast-approaching death, felt himself to be once again in the presence of a loving father. To realize that this is an utterly human event, that the victim freely gave himself to suffering, that he did so for an oft stated purpose, is to realize its extraordinary nature. Libraries have been written trying to express the meaning of Jesus' death. It provides an example of human nature almost beyond comprehension. All other forms of behavior pale before the glory of this sacrificial love. Nothing else that we deem powerful, including human power itself, is as powerful and as profound as this love.

Rarely do we get through life without some significant suffering. In Jesus we see an absolute resolution to engage great suffering, even to the point of momentarily being broken by it, yet at no point does he become the prisoner of his own pain. Again and again he reaches out— to the thief beside him, to his disciple, to his mother, to those who are causing his suffering—asking that they may be forgiven. May such grace be ours in the time of suffering. May we receive a grace enabling us to be a grace to those around us.

NEW LIFE

To an extent much more than many realize, the great rhythm of our lives is from dying to new life. Each night we die into sleep; each morning we rise to new life. A thousand times we will experience these little deaths: the little death of craven fear before some unavoidable experience we must face; the little death of prolonged depression—and in this case word "little" does not deny the terrible cost; the brittle, little deaths of disappointments; the grip of panic, when we may think that we are dying in the most immediate and literal sense.

When we speak of the resurrection of our Lord Jesus Christ, we are naming the mystery that is at the heart of Christian faith. We are also naming something that many Christians in Western culture find difficult to believe. We ask, "How did it happen?"or "What *really* happened?" Such questions are not unreasonable or invalid or a betrayal of Christian faith, but they can never be satisfactorily answered. Although we search the various accounts and record their inconsistencies, the mystery of the resurrection cannot be diminished, and its awe-inspiring power cannot cease to affect the thinking and living of millions of people. Even in the earliest days of the Christian church, believers were not thinking merely in terms of a resuscitated body. In all accounts of the risen Jesus, we are made aware that his presence, though real and immediate, is also mysteriously other. He is present, yet occupying a different realm of reality.

Even trying to say this much is to seek vainly for adequate language. Mary of Magdala is the very first human being to realize that, while she is in the presence of the risen Jesus, she is with him in a way that she cannot understand. She tries literally to grasp him and cannot. But an intellectual grasp is also impossible. We need to emulate her in this and accept her insight and her wisdom. The appearances of the risen Lord deeply affect those who experience them. They are themselves enlivened, their lives are re-energized, their sense of purpose is renewed. We see this in the lives of Mary of Magdala and the apostle Peter. Christian faith promises that it can also be true for us, as well. The resurrection of Jesus is not merely a past event. It is an ever-present reality in the life of the believer.

⊷32⊷

RELATING TO THE PAST

Early on the first day of the week while it was still dark, Mary Magdalene came to the tomb and saw that the stone had been removed from the tomb. So she ran and went to Simon Peter and the other disciple, the one whom Jesus loved, and said to them, "They have taken the Lord out of the tomb, and we do not know where they have laid him."

(from John 20:11–18)

⊷ ⊶

One of the tests of our maturity is the way we relate to the past. To a greater or less degree, our lives are shaped by things that happened in the past. To deny those things, to try to pretend they never happened, is self-defeating. However it is also damaging to refuse to let go of the past, to insist on clinging to it and demanding that things always will stay the same.

We are in the extraordinary hours after our Lord's crucifixion. The small community of disciples and friends is devastated. As in any crisis, human nature shows itself in different ways. One deeply courageous woman decides that she is going to act on her own. Her name is Mary of Magdala. She has led a checkered life. She appears alone on the stage of the gospel. It would seem that Jesus at some stage made a great difference in her life. There is a hint that he may have helped her with some emotional or mental struggle. We meet her at a time when she has been devastated by the death of someone who has come to mean everything to her. Her response is a measure of her courage and resilience. She has just experienced the horror of watching him die by crucifixion. She did not flinch but stayed at the site, watching carefully as Jesus' body was taken down from the cross. She followed those carrying the body and noted where they placed it.

The ext morning, after what must have been a tormenting night, Mary returns alone to the rock tomb. Walking alone in a darkened and deserted city was itself courageous, certainly dangerous for a woman. When she reaches the place, she finds the tomb open. There is no sign of Jesus' body. Deeply distressed, she turns and runs instinctively to where she can find support, the lodgings where some of the disciples are staying. Utterly distraught, she cries out the dreadful news, beseeching them to come and see. Two of them, Peter and John, return with her. Peter examines the tomb, notes some of the details, and begins to grapple with the seemingly impossible. John leaps to the intuition that the impossible has occurred. They both leave.

Mary stays, now once again alone. Hearing a sound she turns and sees a figure. She must have felt extremely vulnerable in this grim and solitary place. Such is her desperation that she walks toward the figure and implores him to tell her where Jesus' body has been taken. At this point she hears her name spoken. Immediately she recognizes the voice she thought lost to her for ever. She cries out the name by which she has known him, and she moves to embrace him. To do so is absolutely instinctive. Unbelievably he is hers again. Yet what Mary wishes cannot be. The same voice that has gently named her speaks now what must have been chilling words. She is told, "Do not hold on to me." She encounters a mystery. She has met not a loved one who has returned from death, but one who has moved beyond death. Only when she faces and acknowledges this new reality will she be able to relate to the person she loves. Only when she acknowledges that the present and the future are utterly different from the past, will she be able to possess a new kind of intimacy with Jesus.

In the first moments of this understanding, Mary turns, goes to the community, and says simply, "I have seen the Lord." There is an extraordinary paradox at the heart of life. We might express it initially as the realization that, to keep anything, we must be ready to let it go. The same is true in our relationships, even those that are deepest. We cannot demand that the present moment be retained in its present form and quality. Only if we are prepared to let it go, fully acknowledging that it is past, can we hope to possess in the present what made the past so precious.

⇥ 33 ⇤

SUPPORTING THE FUTURE

After these things Jesus showed himself again to his disciples by the Sea of Tiberius. Simon Peter said to them, "I am going fishing." They said to him, "We will go with you."...Just after daybreak Jesus stood on the beach; but the disciples did not know it was Jesus. ...When they had gone ashore, they saw a charcoal fire there, with fish on it, and bread. Jesus said to them, "Come and have breakfast."...When they had finished breakfast Jesus said to Simon Peter, "Simon, son of John, do you love me more than these?" He said to him, "Yes Lord, you know that I love you." Jesus said to him, "Feed my lambs."

(John 21:1–19)

⇥ ⇤

All of us have someone to thank for coming to our rescue at a difficult time in life. It may have been a personal crisis that we were not able to face on our own. It may have been a professional crisis, when things looked grim and we simply could not cope. Someone came. We sat with them, maybe ate with them, perhaps even wept with them, but in the end we walked away the better for their support.

It is some weeks after the terrible and mysterious events of Jesus' crucifixion and resurrection. The disciples have returned to Galilee, heading instinctively for home and the familiar world of the lake. They are devastated, deeply depressed, and immobilized. There comes a moment when Peter decides that this pattern must be broken: he is going fishing. We can almost hear the relief in their voices as they go with him. They have a ghastly night. There seem to be no fish in the lake. Dawn comes, and a voice calls to them from the shore. John immediately recognizes the voice. It is Jesus who, with almost studied casualness, offers them a simple breakfast he has prepared.

After a while Jesus calls Peter aside. Jesus asks him no less than three times if Peter loves him. Each time Peter replies, showing increasing indignation at the repeated question. Each time Jesus asks Peter to "tend my lambs, tend my sheep." If we wish to understand what is going on in this intimate moment between Jesus and his most trusted disciple, we have to recall another moment some weeks before. We are in the upper room the night before the trials, the questions, the beatings, and the dying. Jesus looks around the table and says words that must have appalled them. They had just shared the bread and the cup when Jesus announced that one of them will betray him.

At some moment in the ensuing clamor of voices, Jesus says something to Peter that have mystified and hurt him. Jesus said, "Simon, listen! Satan has demanded to sift all of you like wheat, but I have prayed for you that your own faith may not fail; and you, when you have turned back, strengthen your brothers." Peter simply could not hear it. He blustered, "Lord I am ready to go with you to prison and to death!" But Jesus told Peter that he would deny their relationship. And so it happened. Peter *did* deny the relationship again and again, to his own extreme distress. He then carried his guilt home to Galilee. Then comes the encounter with Jesus.

I cannot help thinking that, when Jesus tells Peter to feed his sheep, he is directing Peter toward the care of the other disciples. There will be many others, but now these few are the all-important embryo from which the future will grow. Here on this beach Jesus is putting Peter back together again, restoring his self-esteem, returning to him his leadership of the disciples. Why give back leadership to one who has been broken? Because our Lord, who understands human nature, knows that the capacity for leadership will likely be found where there has been a struggle to survive. To be broken by life, to have persevered and climbed back, can often be a source of great strength and resilience. Not always, of course. Life is never an always. But very often we do see this pattern.

The person who has buckled under strain, who has struggled with themselves and their demons, can become the kind of man or woman who is sensitive to stress in others and able to serve their needs. Leadership is often found among those who have been wounded. That this is so should not surprise us for by grace we know the companionship of One who bears wounds by which we still can recognize him, and because of which we can cry, "My Lord and my God!"

SCRIPTURAL INDEX